# THE CASE OF THE JEALOUS

# Lover

THE CASE OF THE JEALOUS

# Lover

Clifford
L. Frazier

⟎ Whitaker House

Unless otherwise indicated, all Scripture quotations are from the *New American Standard Bible*, © 1960, 1962, 1968, 1971, 1973, 1975, 1977 by The Lockman Foundation. Used by permission.

Scripture quotations marked (NKJV) are taken from the *New King James Version*, © 1979, 1980, 1982 by Thomas Nelson, Inc. Used by permission. All rights reserved.

Scripture quotations marked (KJV) are taken from the *King James Version* of the Bible.

Scripture quotations marked (TLB) are from *The Living Bible*, © 1971 by Tyndale House Publishers, Wheaton, Illinois. Used by permission.

## THE CASE OF THE JEALOUS LOVER

ISBN: 0-88368-547-7
Printed in the United States of America
Copyright © 1999 by Clifford L. Frazier

Whitaker House
30 Hunt Valley Circle
New Kensington, PA 15068

Library of Congress Cataloging-in-Publication Data

Frazier, Clifford L., 1951–
        The case of the jealous lover / by Clifford L. Frazier.
                p.   cm.
        ISBN 0-88368-547-7 (trade paper : alk. paper)
        1. Jesus Christ—Miscellanea. 2. Frazier, Clifford L., 1951–
I. Title.
BT295.F73    1998
232—DC21                                        98-27898

1 2 3 4 5 6 7 8 9 10 11 12 13 / 07 06 05 04 03 02 01 00 99

# *Contents*

# Dedication

*This book is dedicated to
my loving parents,
Francis A. and Ida E. Frazier.
They are now resting in the arms of
a Jealous Lover.*

# *Acknowledgments*

T he efforts and support of others are the secret ingredients of my success. To be thankful for the same is the secret to having a good character. I thank the Lord Jesus Christ who rescued me and continues to hold me in His arms. I also offer many thanks to Mr. and Mrs. Marcelle and Ann Perry for their inspiration and assistance.

I do so appreciate Bishop T. D. Jakes, a man of excellence and a man with the gift of bringing people together who would otherwise never meet. His special gift to me was his persistent attempt to move me from "I ought to" to "I did it." Thank you, Bishop.

I must make a special effort to thank my editors, Ms. Wendi Thomas and Mrs. Karen Hadley. Wendi and Karen, you remind me of the wisdom of Ecclesiastes 11:1: *"Cast your bread upon the waters, for you will find it after many days"* (NKJV).

One of my chief blessings is the love and support of my two daughters, Leah and Janelle. They read my drafts and cheered me on. They are precious young women whom I love with all my heart. Of course, I saved the best for last. I call her Mama, but she is my wife, best friend, and greatest cheerleader. Her name is Pamela J. Frazier; she's highly anointed and the joy of my life.

# *Introduction*

*T*he *Case of the Jealous Lover* was born out of a deep desire of mine to represent God's side of the salvation story—His motivations, desires, and interest in us. We always hear what He has done for us. What does God receive by winning us to Himself? In an effective and workable relationship, there must be mutual benefit, communication, sharing, and oneness.

Most believers know the details of the Lord's blessings in their lives. They can make long lists of the many things He has done for them. Do we, however, as believers, spend the same amount of time listing all the things God receives from being related to us? Do we tell Him how much we love Him when we're not trying to get something from

Him? When we pray, are there times when we never ask Him for things but spend our prayer time telling Him how good He is to us? These courtesies are all a part of having a good relationship. A human relationship that didn't have back-and-forth communication, sharing, and love would soon dissolve.

God refers to Himself with names of love throughout the Bible. It is interesting that, with as much time and language as God uses to describe Himself as the Lover of our souls, we hardly think of Him in that way.

In Exodus 34:14, the Lord introduces Himself as the Jealous Lover of Israel: *"For you shall not worship any other god, for the LORD, whose name is Jealous, is a jealous God."* Notice that He uses love language. He declares that He has strong feelings for His bride, the church.

When I first read this verse, the term *jealous* applied to the Lord was unsettling for me. I wondered how He could associate Himself with such a negative term. My answer was soon to follow.

I studied the word *jealous*. It means "having a strong passion for one's own possessions." But even after studying the meaning of the word *jealous,* my spirit was still unsettled. I investigated further, and the result is this book, the record of my discoveries.

# Introduction

Several years ago, I preached a message entitled, "What's in It for God?" The premise of that sermon was similar to that of this book. I felt that I needed to speak up for God, to be a champion of His grace and sovereignty.

We know from the Scriptures that God is sovereign and that He created all things. Knowing this, you may ask, "If God is sovereign and has the power to speak things into existence, why did Christ have to die for us? Couldn't He just have declared us righteous and been done with it?"

There are some real mysteries associated with this message. Why did Christ die? Couldn't He have better served the kingdom alive? What good did His death do? And if His death was required to pay for our redemption, wasn't the price too high?

Of course, anything is possible with God. But the fact that He didn't redeem man a different way indicates that a different plan wouldn't have been effective. Our God never operates inefficiently, and He never makes mistakes.

My purpose in this book is to present the message of the Cross from God's point of view. In order to carry out this purpose, I have presented two stories. In the first part of this book, I establish our creation in God and His tender love for us. I also offer my own testimony about how I came to understand this amazing love. The second part of this book is an allegorical story that I hope will help you understand and receive God's love.

The style of *The Case of the Jealous Lover* is different from other commentaries. I blended elements of a mystery novel with practical studies of the spiritual lessons. Many of the chapters contain the drama of the jealous lover followed by a practical application of the Scriptures.

This is my first book, and I pray that you will be blessed by it. You decide if the approach works. If it does, give Jesus the glory. My prayer is that *The Case of the Jealous Lover* will bless you and encourage you to grow in the Lord and to love Him more.

—CLIFFORD L. FRAZIER

# Part One

*Chapter One*

# *The Touch of God*

*Chapter One*

# The Touch of God

*Then the LORD God formed man of dust
from the ground, and breathed into his nostrils
the breath of life; and man became a living being.
—Genesis 2:7*

W e begin the story with the beginning of man. The Bible tells us clearly that God created man for His glory (Isaiah 43:7) and that *"all things have been created by Him and for Him"* (Colossians 1:16). There is no doubt that He created man out of love. God—the all-powerful, all-knowing, everywhere-at-once God who sits high and looks low (Psalm 33:13–15)—created everything by the power of His words alone. We read in Psalm 33:6, *"By the word of the LORD the heavens were made, and by the breath of His mouth all their host."*

Unlike man, who has to create with building materials, God created all that exists out of absolutely nothing. For man there must be some kind of raw substance from which things are made. But when God creates, He simply speaks things into existence.

He speaks, and atoms are created, and at the same time those atoms are blended together with other atoms to form molecules. Those molecules are bonded to other molecules to form components that are the building blocks of life. Everything that exists contains these components.

The wonder of God's creation is that He can speak and the resulting creation is without error the first time—every time. He needs no structural engineer to approve His design. He doesn't consult a designer to discover whether blue and green are compatible colors.

He speaks, and the wonder of creation appears. He speaks, and a brown cow begins to eat green grass and give white milk.

He speaks, and there is water to drink. This odorless and tasteless liquid is consumed and reported to be good, for everything that God created is good. (See Genesis 1:31.) All of God's creation except humanity owes its existence to this phenomenon of the creative spoken word of God.

Human beings are not the products of God's spoken word. God radically departed from His previous method of creation when He decided to make people.

## *The Creation of Man*

When God decided to make man, He did so not only as an artist but also as a passionate lover. I imagine Him taking on a visible form, perhaps like His appearances in the Old Testament—His *theophanies*—when He appeared to people as a man or as "the angel of the Lord." I see Him stepping on the earth that He had created and bending over some dirt. He could have, in a nanosecond, spoken a man-form into existence. He had spoken giraffes, aardvarks, and orangutans into existence in a moment, but this would be a different process of creation.

I imagine God using His hands like a sculptor to form man out of the dust of the ground. Reading the biblical account, one can almost feel the tender care with which He fashioned the human body.

Carefully molding the head, placing eye sockets in the front of the skull, He ensured that this creature would have three-dimensional sight. He might have been saying to Himself, "Man will not only be able to see that something is out there, he will also be able to know the depth and distance of that something just by looking. Most importantly, I want him to see Me face to face."

Notice the order of God's creation. He made the majestic mountains, the lush valleys, the sparkling rivers, and the cascading waterfalls before He made man. He created graceful birds of the air and powerful beasts of the field before He made man. God did so because He wanted man to see all that He had created, to be impressed, and to say so. Creation was and is a dazzling display of design.

God also fashioned ears designed to capture distinct sounds from the air. For instance, man's ears can distinguish between the vibrations of melody and danger. One can imagine God thinking, "I want him to hear the sound of My voice. Also, the symphony of sound produced by My birds and other animals will be for his enjoyment. He will hear and bless Me for it."

God created a brain for man. This is not simply a network of nerve endings, but a complex computer capable of performing extraordinary tasks. The power to conceive, to develop procedures, to have independent thought, to reason, to solve problems, to analyze, to express ideas, and to invent things was invested in this brain. No other earthly creature has this combined capability.

God programmed all of His other creatures with instinct, not reason. This was part of His design. These creatures can't help praising and glorifying God—one way or another—by their very existence.

But to humanity, God gave the gift of free will. Human beings can think thoughts and express ideas that may or may not glorify their Creator. Why? Because God wants us to love Him freely, not because we have to. What a thought! God, who is self-sufficient, all-knowing, and everywhere at once, wants our love.

Being loved is the essence of life. It is the purest gift anyone can give another individual. God wanted to create beings in His image whom He could love and who would return His love.

It is easy for the animals, the wind, the waves, and the atmosphere to obey God. No other alternatives exist for them. But a man can bless God or curse Him, honor Him or blaspheme Him, adore Him or despise Him—and when he dishonors God, he often lives to tell the story.

Is this a flaw in God's design?

No! It is a display of His passionate love for us.

God is willing to risk the pain of rejection for the pleasure of real love. Love cannot come to those who are unwilling to be hurt. The expression of real love cannot be forced; it must be freely given. You cannot make a person love you and speak soothing words of devotion. You can force people to recite a script or to repeat phrases, but that is not love.

It cannot move God emotionally to hear a dog bark when He knows that the dog is doing what its nature requires. But when a person, equipped to discover, analyze, evaluate, and decide, reaches out for God as though reaching out for a father, and says to God, "I love you"—that moves God.

I believe that it was the thought of having someone to appreciate Him for who He is and what He does that caused God to create man in the first place.

The most impressive expression of God's love during His creation of man was what He did last. It was the way He gave life to the man He had formed.

The hands of God molded and fashioned the body of that first man. I imagine that, as His hands went over the skeletal form, they caused skin to fall into place. When God finished, He undoubtedly paused to look at His creation. It was flawless in design and unique in its features, but it was lifeless.

Then He did something so awesome that the angels must have taken note of it. The Scriptures report that God made man in His image and after His likeness (Genesis 1:26) and breathed into man the breath of life (Genesis 2:7). How did He do it? Some theologians believe that the Scriptures imply that God "spread Himself out" on that sculptured clay model, as if placing Himself eye to eye, mouth to mouth, chest to chest, legs to legs. It was almost as if He was making a copy of Himself. He covered the body of man and blew into him the breath of life.

When that man opened his eyes to life, the first thing he beheld was God. Imagine waking up and seeing God before your eyes! With that one act, the great God of heaven demonstrated His special love for man.

The love of God abides with believers even now through the indwelling of the Holy Spirit (Romans 5:5). It has never been the attitude of God to be distant, cold, or uncaring—especially not to those He has created and redeemed.

God's way of creating man was personal and immediate. He touched man and breathed life into him. God continues to touch our lives today and meet out spiritual, physical, and emotional needs.

## The Case of the Jealous Lover

### The Gift of God's Touch

One of the best gifts human love brings is the act of touching. It is sometimes called caressing or stroking. A touch speaks without words. Similarly, a spiritual touch from God tells us that He is very near to us.

Sometimes a baby cries, not because of hunger or distress, but because of the need to be held. Young children will run up to their parents with uplifted hands, reaching for them. They are saying, essentially, "Pick me up and hold me. I feel safe in your arms."

God loves us so much that His creative, soothing hands still touch us in all our situations. He wants us to reach for Him; He wants to pick us up when we are crying.

He doesn't merely speak life to us; He breathes it into every fiber of our beings. He comforts and reassures us by His touch. In a word, He is there for us.

One of the most striking illustrations of God's tender care and desire to touch us is found in the eighth chapter of Matthew:

*And when* [Jesus] *had come down from the mountain, great multitudes followed Him.*

## The Touch of God

> *And behold, a leper came to Him, and bowed down to Him, saying, "Lord, if You are willing, You can make me clean." And He stretched out His hand and touched him, saying, "I am willing; be cleansed." And immediately his leprosy was cleansed.*
>
> *(Matthew 8:1–3)*

Much of the time, when Jesus healed, He did so by speaking to the condition. But when the man with leprosy came to Him, Jesus did not simply speak healing to him. Instead, Jesus touched him.

This is an intense example of love because people with leprosy were considered unclean, and leprosy was considered incurable. No one could go near lepers, let alone touch them. In the days of Christ, lepers were required to announce their arrival when they did come around other people. This would give people an opportunity to keep their distance. Even today, lepers in many countries have to keep away from the general population.

In Bible times, therefore, contracting leprosy was like having a physical and emotional death sentence handed to you. But Jesus showed His love to the leper not only by healing him, but also by saying with His touch, "Your condition is not too bad for Me."

Jesus was saying, "I love you enough to risk contracting what you have in order to give you what I have. I love you enough to care about your feelings and to cover your shame." This is real love.

When that healed leper left his encounter with Jesus and was asked what happened, he must have replied, "He touched me."

## God's Personal Involvement

Sprinkled throughout the Scriptures are examples of this kind of personal involvement on the part of God. Another example of His touch of love is found in the story of the Shunammite woman. (See 2 Kings 4:8–37.)

The Shunammite was a woman of some prominence in her community. Known and respected where business was conducted in the city, she still had something missing in her life that made it incomplete: she was childless.

This was a terrible disgrace for women during her time. She made the best of it, though, by busying herself with the family business and serving God.

Her faithfulness in providing for the prophet Elisha's needs was rewarded with a promise from

God, given through the prophet: "You shall have a son." (See verse 16.) Could she truly have joy after all these years of disappointment? Could she now hold her head high and give a gift to her husband?

She had accepted her condition; she had not asked for a son. But God's love is so precious. He considers all of our needs. He gave her what she wanted but would not ask for. And just as God had promised, she gave birth to a son.

The Bible offers no information about the child until he was almost grown. One day he was working in the field with his father. It was an ordinary day. Suddenly, without warning, the boy began to complain of a pain in his head. The father ordered a servant to carry the son home. The son was brought to his mother, but it was only a few hours before he died on his mother's lap.

To have what you have always hoped for taken away is much harder to deal with than never having it at all. One can easily imagine the mother crying out, "How could this happen? Lord, You promised me this child. Now my son has preceded me to the grave. What do we do now? This is horrible!"

The boy represented the hope and future of her family. He was the source of their joy. Now, as if a cruel joke were being played on them, his life was snuffed out.

## The Case of the Jealous Lover

How many times have we faced bewildering situations that shook our foundations? We have wondered, "Could life get any more difficult?"

Anyone who has experienced the loss of a loved one knows how difficult life can be for those who are left behind. Nothing is more final than death—unless Love stands in the way.

The Shunammite woman knew that God would find a way. When the boy died on her lap, she put the lifeless child in the room that had been prepared for Elisha. She then went searching for the prophet.

When she found him, she fell at his feet and reminded him that he had promised her a son. He had promised her when she hadn't even asked, and now she needed his help.

Elisha, who in this story represents the care of God, first sent his servant, Gehazi, to deal with the situation. Gehazi came back and reported that he was unsuccessful in raising the boy to life.

Then Elisha went to her house. He found the boy in the room reserved for him. While praying to God, Elisha lay on that child and covered him from head to toe. Life came back into that boy's body. He was restored to his family. God's love found a way.

The first lesson to be learned from this story is that God will go to great lengths to show His love. There are some situations in our lives in which a word from God will suffice. Then there are times when we need Him to lay Himself over our situations. We need His personal involvement, His touch; we need the hand of the Lord upon us.

Second, this story teaches us that if death cannot stop the love of God, our other problems are not too great for Him either. If the love of God can bring life out of death, His love can also bring joy out of sorrow, peace out of confusion, and laughter out of sadness. If death cannot stop God, then a wayward child, a financial mountain, a confused mind, or a hopeless cause cannot stop Him. Reach for Him, and you, too, will be able to say, "He touched me."

\* \* \*

As a foundation for this book, we have seen how God created man and loves him in a passionate way. We have seen how God touches man at his point of need. But the greatest manifestation of God's love and personal commitment to us is Christ coming to the earth to live and to suffer and die for us. It is His incredible love in dying for us that is the main focus of this book. In the following pages, we will explore the depths of this love.

*The Case of the Jealous Lover*

## A PRAYER

*Dear Lord, I pray for the precious soul who has just read this chapter. Maybe he, too, is looking for love and needs a touch from You. Maybe his situation seems hopeless or his condition untouchable.*

*But I know, Lord, that You care for him and love him. Touch him now. Let Your hands of compassion soothe him right where he is.*

*Lay Yourself upon his problems if You have to. Most of all, let him rest in Your love.*

*In Jesus' name, I pray. Let it be so.*

*Chapter Two*

# *Growing Up*

*Chapter Two*

# *Growing Up*

*I* was born into a family that embraced the Bible as the infallible Word of God without question. Going to church was as regular an activity as going to work, having dinner, or playing a game. We went on Wednesday night, Friday night, and Sunday morning; and during revivals we went all week long and on Sunday nights. This was the routine, and it continued throughout the formative years of my life.

There was never a question in anyone's mind, except maybe my father's, that when Sunday came we were going to church. My father was never antagonistic toward church, but he was definitely not in the fold. He was one of the few people in my life who did not accept the teachings of the church without question. He had many questions, the answers to which came too late for him. Fortunately, they did not come too late for me.

After several years of churchgoing, I knew the church doctrine well. I clearly understood that there were only two possible destinations for the souls of men: heaven or hell. I studied my memory verses, won the Sunday school contests, recited the special event poems and readings, and dutifully baby-sat the younger children in the church.

With religious fervor, the church of my youth stressed the message of the Lord's return with all its ramifications. I knew the details of what life would be like immediately after the Rapture. I had an almost encyclopedic knowledge of the effects of fire and brimstone on the body and how completely miserable people would be when they experienced the wrath of God. I could feel the radiant heat of hell's fires and developed spiritual blisters after each service. I was tormented by thoughts of dying without Christ.

My church's zealous devotion to practical holiness was its chief asset. God was not to be toyed with. *"Do not be deceived, God is not mocked"* (Galatians 6:7) was the motto of the church. I learned what couldn't be worn and what couldn't adorn or be affixed to the body. I knew all the fun places that couldn't be entered and what colors were inappropriate for true believers to wear.

What I really knew was that it was going to be a real miracle if I made it to heaven! The church doctrine had the effect of terrifying me instead of drawing me to Jesus as my Savior. If *"the fear of the LORD* [is] *the beginning of wisdom"* (Psalm 111:10), I was a genius. Unfortunately, I had the wrong kind of fear of God.

By the time I entered college, this fear had taken its toll on me. I was a wreck emotionally. I replaced the blisters with calluses. When I heard hellfire sermons, they didn't move me like they used to. I could endure Judgment-Day preaching because I had become almost numb to it.

The intrigue of college life quickly diluted the potency of my church upbringing. I was mesmerized by the articulate speeches of my professors and their adroitness in expressing alternative philosophies. The once-forbidden dances and social events were calling my name. I answered every call. I was too scared to get into drugs. I did, however, pop a few pills just to be sure I could say I had done it.

I was out from under the control of the church, but the freedom wasn't what I expected. I still constantly thought about church, and the knowledge that I was not saved began to affect me. Now I was in a predicament. I was scared to go to church and scared not to.

God sent a wonderful Christian lady to my rescue. She was about sixty years old and took an interest in my salvation. Though her beliefs were strict, she showed me love and concern in a fresh way. She was from the old school, which means that she believed in very conservative values and religious practices.

The exact nature of the old school remains unclear to me, but I know this woman graduated from it. Her beliefs were like the ones my old church preached: almost everything that was fun was sinful. But when this lady ministered to me, her manner was soothing. Her prompting moved me to get serious about seeking God.

Many months later, I had a real salvation experience. After years of learning the doctrinal specifics of how to be saved, I finally understood the truth of what Christ did for me at Calvary and was able to apply that work to my life. This brought me back to church, but things were still much the same. The negative teachings, and the emphasis on hell and the consequences of living a sinful life, were still the main points of the sermons that were preached. I did have a bit more freedom in how I would incorporate these teaching into my life, however, because I was older and pretty much on my own.

I felt the call of God to the ministry and focused all my attention on following that call. Yet the pastor and other ministers at the church were stingy with their help. When I went to my pastor for advice on how to prepare for the ministry, he told me to study the books of the Bible concerned with all the prophets and all the kings. I was devastated. Why didn't he help me? He acted as if the details of Christian ministry were trade secrets. I expected my pastor to become a mentor for me, teaching me the mechanics of sermon preparation. I had looked forward to being his ministry disciple. I thought he would take me with him to his out-of-town preaching engagements. At the very least, I thought that he would recommend a course of study, a seminary, or a Bible school, or would give me a bibliography of theological books to read. He did none of the above.

He wasn't the only one who treated me this way. I sought out other preachers, hoping that they would take me under their wings. But they gave me the cold-shoulder treatment, too.

What was wrong? They all made me feel as if I was being subjected to a baptism by fire: if I could withstand their best efforts to discourage me, then I could be a preacher.

But I did not give up, and I later learned that they didn't answer my questions because they themselves did not know the answers. They, too, had had to face the baptism by fire from their pastors and had passed on the legacy of bad habits, procedures, and policies.

Years passed, and I started a church just like the strict, legalistic, negative church I'd grown up knowing—until, one day, I had a rendezvous with God.

## *A Rendezvous with God*

It was a crisp, cold Saturday morning in winter. I was going fishing with one of the deacons of the church, a personal friend. We knew that the fish were biting early in the morning. My friend had a special spot that no one else knew about where we were guaranteed to catch fish.

Off we went to Lake Tawakani. We sat on the side of the bridge overlooking the peaceful, deep blue waters of the lake. Our lines were in the water—an invitation to all interested fish to come and dine.

My wife, safely sleeping at home, was pregnant with our second child. She didn't know where I was. No one knew where I was. There was no one on the bridge with us, and there were very few cars traveling by.

Soon we were in deep discussions about everything. We talked about homes and families, the church, our goals for the future. We just talked.

All the talk was nice, but I needed to catch some fish. I looked out and saw some reeds sticking up out of the water. I knew if I could just get my line out to those reeds, I would catch fish. I told my friend as much.

I reeled in my line, checked the bait, and stood precariously on the edge of the bridge with my toes pointing down. I cocked my arm back to give maximum force to the cast. I cast the line.

The bait went in, the line went in, the pole went in, and then I went in!

I fell off the bridge into twenty feet of ice-cold water. The peaceful surface of the lake could not have warned me that, just where I fell in, there was an underwater current that could drag me right to the middle of the lake. I did not know how to swim, tread water, or float. I also had on thermal underwear, layers of outer coverings, and combat boots, all of which made it even more difficult to stay above the surface.

There I was, suddenly in the water, in the winter, without a hope of survival. Instantly, the thought ran through my mind, "The kid is gone!"

Fortunately, I didn't have that life-flashing-before-my-eyes experience. Instead, I just hung in the water, oblivious to the effects of hypothermia on my body.

My friend, Brother Arthur, acted immediately. He jumped into the icy waters, swam over to me, put his arm around my shoulder, and said, "Be calm!"

"Be calm?" I thought. "I'm dying in this water, and he wants me to be calm."

Suddenly, he disappeared under the water.

At the time, I didn't know that the icy water was rapidly cooling my body. I didn't know that, before long, I could go into a state of shock and lose mobility and rationality. Without warning, I could just give up and pass out.

I was hanging in the water. Water was in my nose and mouth, but I never went under the lake's surface—quite astounding for someone who did not know how to swim.

I felt myself dying. My field of vision was fading like the picture at the end of a cartoon show does. All that was left was a little circle of light like the one in which Porky Pig used to appear saying: "That's all, folks!"

Then, into my little circle of light an old man appeared. He said four of the most blessed words a human ear can hear: "I will save you!" At that moment, a peace that contradicted the obvious danger I was in came over me, and I wasn't afraid to die.

To this day, I do not know where this man came from, if not from heaven. Remember, there were no people anywhere in sight when this event began.

This old man wasn't in a boat but was carrying a boat rope. He threw the rope to me. It was just long enough to reach me.

I grabbed the rope and pulled. He said, "Don't you pull; I'll pull you." And pull he did. He pulled me through the water with the rope and then pulled me up onto shore with his hands.

At that time, I weighed 240 pounds, completely dry, and now I was quite wet. This little old man pulled me out of the water by my coat collar as if I were a little child or a puppy dog.

After I was safely on the shore, I looked back over the water. I could not see my friend or any sign that he was struggling to survive. The water was calm again. I was safe, but what about my friend? All I could think about was what I would tell his wife.

I didn't have time for long, fancy prayers. I didn't have time to warm up to God. My prayer had to be succinct and to the point. I prayed, "Lord Jesus, Brother Arthur!"

When I finished that prayer, Brother Arthur shot out of the water like a rocket ship shooting for the stars. Water came out of his mouth, and he cried, "Jesus!" Then he went back down under the water. This happened three times.

By this time, more people had gathered on the bridge. Apparently we had attracted the attention of some passersby. A chain of men formed on the slope of the shore to help my friend emerge from the water.

Just as they were about to reach him, one of the volunteers broke from the chain and jumped into the water. The cold water immobilized him, and he had to be pulled from the water along with Brother Arthur. Finally, when everyone was safe, we all gathered on the bridge.

The old man stood like a sentinel and watched as some of us cared for my friend.

I got up, searching for money to pay this man for saving my life. I found some soggy bills and gratefully handed them to him.

He refused to accept the money. He looked at me and said, "Just do something good for somebody else."

When I looked down to check on my friend's condition and looked back up again, the old man was gone. No car was driving away from the bridge, and there was no place for this man to hide. In an instant, he had disappeared.

Many times since that experience, I've tried to analyze the day I almost died. I learned how to swim and tried to duplicate how I had hung in the water. I sank every time.

I am convinced that the Lord sent two angels to rescue me that day. One angel, whom I could see, was pulling me out of the water. The other one, whom I couldn't see, was holding me up in the water.

Isn't that just like the Lord? He not only cares about getting a person out of danger but also about preserving him or her in the midst of the danger.

As awesome as the event was, the most significant part of the experience was the long-range effect it had on my life. The thought of death lost its terrorizing effect on me. Most of all, I recognized the real value of salvation.

To know that you are saved and that everything is right between you and the Lord—even when you are facing death—is so reassuring. I discovered just how much the Lord cares for me.

Why did it take me all that time to discover this? Well, I think that maybe it's not as obvious as it seems. I had heard all the "God loves you" sentences, but too much of my time had been spent on theological issues rather than on relationship issues—on developing a personal relationship with God. The words were there, but the relationship was not. It was not that God wasn't reaching for me; it was that I knew more *about* Him than I knew Him in a personal way. I could talk about Him only as a subject to be explored, not as a person I was close to. But He had saved my life at Lake Tawakani. I knew it and loved Him for it.

For the first time in my life, I understood that God loves me. It wasn't "God loves people" or "God loves the world" or even "God is love." It was, God loves *me*. What a revelation!

I look back on that event and realize how significant it was for my spiritual life. Actually, there have been two major fork-in-the-road spiritual experiences for me during my life. The first one was my near-death experience described above. The second one was going to seminary after growing up in the church, pastoring a few years, and being very much settled in my own theological position.

The changes these two experiences had on my life were dramatic. They made me redefine the connection between myself and God. I learned from these events that what God really wants is for us to know Him.

To make this point even clearer, let me tell you about my seminary experience.

*Chapter Three*

# *Cemetery—Oops! I Mean Seminary!*

*Chapter Three*

# Cemetery—Oops!
# I Mean Seminary!

*T*he worship services, special concerts, and other events; the politics and society, the rules, and the doctrine of the church—all of these are meaningless if you do not have a love relationship with God.

Could it be that, after years of dutifully attending church and intensely memorizing Scripture, I'd missed that point? After years of annual Easter sermons about the Cross and the intense sufferings of Christ, was I still ignorant of His purpose in dying?

"It couldn't be," I thought. I was always ready to fight for the cause of Christ. I knew all the enemies of the Lord and would give my life to prove them wrong. But God used an encounter with one of these enemies to begin the process of renewing my attitudes toward Him.

One day, one of the enemies engaged me in debate. I was prepared to do battle. This person was not saved, and I knew it.

I understood that my Christian duty was to defend the faith against all enemies, foreign and domestic (translation: blatant sinners and so-called Christian sinners). After a few minutes of championship debate, my opponent asked me, "Where did you get your theological ideas from?" He added, "If you knew the original languages, you would not hold these positions." I felt derailed.

I knew I was right, but I couldn't prove it to this person. I decided then that I would find a seminary and attend just long enough to become comfortable in the Greek and Hebrew languages. Then, I thought, I would be able to prove my points from the original languages. There would be no stopping me.

I found a seminary that specialized in teaching biblical languages. I went in and told them that they could keep all their other courses and that I was only interested in learning the Greek language.

I didn't tell them so, but my church upbringing had prepared me for the apparent tricks of the Devil in seminaries. I remember countless times hearing preachers of my persuasion saying things like, "Don't let these educated fools going to the cemetery—oops! I mean seminary—tell you anything. You'd better let the Holy Spirit teach you."

I ate up that kind of teaching, and so did those around me who shared my enthusiasm for the truth. It made so much sense to us. All one needed was the Bible and the Holy Spirit. The Bible was God's Word, and the Holy Spirit was the only Interpreter needed.

We were taught that having other Bible study books was a hindrance to real spiritual growth. Just recounting these things is embarrassing to me.

We were so sincere, too! We thought that we were an oasis of truth in the desert of Christian heresy. What we really felt was that we were the only ones who were truly saved. It was pitiful, I know, but that was our mind-set.

I am sure my own attitude showed. My air of superiority, fostered by my "special revelation knowledge," must have been obvious.

The dean of the college, however, was so gracious and kind to me. He never pushed the point or required me to renounce my views. He very gently steered me from one course to another.

I started out with one Greek course. I devoured it. Then the dean said, "Why don't you try the Nature of God course?" His suggestion was an act of God. Taking that course, for me, was like getting saved all over again. I found God!

I know it was He who found me, but bear with me on this. I heard words like *sovereignty, purpose, election,* and *justification*—wonderful words of life. I watched as the professor pored over Scripture after Scripture.

Divine light flooded my blinded soul. I forgot that I was an oasis in the desert of heresy. I discovered that my soul was thirsty for the living water of God.

On one particular day, I watched as the eyes of the "unsaved" professor filled with tears of devotion as he tenderly explained the text. His lip quivered, and he paused, the Scriptures having made him lose his composure. This man wasn't supposed to be saved, but he loved God. He acted as I acted when touched by the Word.

I was so confused. What I saw and felt at school did not line up with what I had been taught in my local church since childhood. There were too many contradictions. For the first time in my saved life, I was not sure that what I had believed for years was valid any longer.

When I left class that day, I also left my theological position. It turned out that my position was not theological at all. For all those years, I had been a student of the teachers and not a student of the Word. My position had been molded by my teachers' traditions.

Years of negativism and pride had taken its toll on my life. I am sure there are some people who are still distrustful of God today because of my pushy, legalistic methods of soulwinning.

I pray that God will have mercy on me because of my ignorance. I do not wish to be too harsh on the church of my childhood, however. The pastors and teachers there did introduce me to Jesus and taught me as well as they could. The problem was that they, too, were victims of a system that revered personal piety over God's grace. It makes me wonder, how many "dead bodies" lie strewn in the wake of the church's evangelistic efforts?

I continued my studies. I became a full-time student and completed my master's degree at the seminary.

Every day when I came home, my wife would ask me, "What do we believe today?" It was so funny. After I learned that I didn't know everything about God, I started questioning all my beliefs.

The process of redefining my theology continued until my last year in seminary.

Then one night, while I was in a deep sleep, I dreamed that I heard a voice saying, "Set free!" I woke up and sat straight up in the bed. My wife thought I was choking. I told her I'd been set free.

Soon after that night, I set up a retreat for the men of my church. At that meeting, I taught them what I'd learned, and the bondage of my previous teaching and rules was undone. I set them free!

One of my ministers quite respectfully asked me, "Pastor, this is different from what you taught us last year. Which is right, what you taught us last year or what you're teaching us this year?"

I replied to him that I had given them the best I had last year, and I was giving them the best I had this year. After the retreat, I went back to the church and set my church free.

What I taught my church then is what I want to teach you now. May the following chapters display for you a God who loves you and wants to have a covenant relationship with you.

I introduce you to the case of the jealous lover....

*Chapter Four*

# A Jealous God

*Chapter Four*

# *A Jealous God*

T he Gospel announces that Jesus Christ *"came into the world to save sinners"* (1 Timothy 1:15). This statement is used around the world to persuade people to come to God. The salvation message is filled with the stories of Christ's death at Calvary, His burial in a borrowed grave, His descent into the realm of Satan, and His taking of the keys of death, hell, and the grave. It's the story of Jesus' victory over death on our behalf. It is such a wonderful message.

But one question remains: Why? Why was the death of Jesus required? Why was it such a horrible death, so brutal and vicious?

## The Case of the Jealous Lover

Christ's death wasn't a clean, clinical euthanasia. It was torturous; it was savage. Christ didn't go quickly while He was sleeping. He died on a cross, friendless and alone, and then had a spear thrust into His side. His heavenly Father's back was the last thing He saw before His head fell in death.

Imagine a criminologist coming on this scene—Jesus dead on the cross, bludgeoned and battered. The criminologist's job is to develop a profile on whoever killed the Christ. This death came from someone's deep feelings of hatred. Who could do such a thing, and why this way?

Let's explore these vital questions through an allegory of the life of Christ that will illustrate, in a dramatic way, Christ's deep love for us—a love that conquered even death. Through this unfolding story, our questions will be answered and a case will be solved: the case of the jealous lover.

This case is filled with mystery, intrigue, passion, and death. But surprisingly, at the heart of it all, is a beautiful love story. This is not the story of a casual acquaintance, but of a strong and passionate devotion. It is not *amore,* a superficial romantic love. It is *agape,* a love that originates from the Lover and is given to the beloved without any conditions. It is the story of the never ending affection God has for the apple of

His eye—for His people, for you! But let's start at the beginning....

* * *

Like a romance novel, the story of the jealous lover begins with a young man, a firstborn prince in a great kingdom, who has found someone special to love. The suitor, filled with excitement, prepares to take her to himself as a wife. He works hard to ensure that she will enjoy his provisions. Everything must be perfect, and he spares no expense. He builds a special place where they will spend their time together.

The gardens are manicured with meticulous care. They are filled with all kinds of fruit-bearing trees, selected especially for their beauty and bounty. "She will love this place," he says to himself.

He can see in his mind's eye all the wonderful evenings they will share. Nothing else he has will compare to the joy this new love in his life will bring. It feels so right, this love he has. Nothing could go wrong, he believes.

But then she leaves him. The story turns into a tragic and classic case of a one-sided love affair. It merits the question usually asked by observers, "Why does it seem as though the good ones always get hooked up with the bad ones?"

## The Case of the Jealous Lover

Sadly, a despised and rejected jealous lover is driven to extreme measures in his attempts to prove his love. Over and over he tries all kinds of things to win the absolute loyalty and exclusive devotion of the one he loves. Yet again and again, the love of his life seems eager to leave him for another.

Her infidelity is hard enough to deal with, but the insult of her choice is worse. She doesn't leave him for another of equal stature. She chooses to be with a low-down, bankrupt, over-the-hill, convicted con artist—a trickster. A rogue who is rotten to the core, he doesn't know what love is, and he couldn't care less about her. In fact, he only wants to be with her long enough to get back at the one who truly loves her. The trickster hates the jealous lover and can find no better way to torment him than to destroy his heart's desire.

Something happened a long time ago between the trickster and the father of the jealous lover. They used to be close, until this tempter's true character emerged. Now the jealous lover has a close relationship with the father, and the trickster hates him for it. The trickster was proven to be a thief and a robber, a liar from the beginning and hell-bent on destroying everything good and decent.

The jealous lover, who has great authority in his father's kingdom, is the champion of righteousness and justice. This rebel could not remain unchecked. The jealous lover and his father were left with no alternative but to expel the thieving trickster from their domain. They stripped him of his exalted position, exposed him as the rogue that he was, and restricted his territory and his power.

The thought of that destroyed relationship with the father and the humiliation that the public banishment has brought to the trickster keep his hatred alive. Oh, he hates the jealous lover with a perfect hatred. It so provokes him that he can hardly think about anything else.

Nearly insane and determined to pay the jealous lover back, he feels he has to find a way to even the score. Being outmatched in power means that a face-to-face confrontation with the jealous lover is out of the question. "But there are other ways," the trickster says to himself.

He calls his little gang together to strategize. He tracks all the movements of the jealous lover and finds out who has his eye. Then he attempts to frustrate all his plans. "I will make your life so miserable that you will wish you'd left me alone," he promises.

The jealous lover knows that something will have to be done about this sorry excuse for a man. The rivalry must end. The universe is not suited for the both of them. This time the trickster would not be demoted; his power would be destroyed.

## The Case of the Jealous Lover

But what about the jealous lover's true love? The jealous lover wonders why his precious one would leave him for someone who absolutely does not care about her. Jealousy—a strong, intense feeling and desire for one's own possession—fills his heart. All he wants is what rightfully belongs to him. His active mind burns with fierce thoughts of anger, rage, and pain.

He is angry because his best efforts to keep his bride have been met with equally strong attempts by her to flee from him. He is enraged because of the irony of this love. How could he give so much to someone, yet she remain cold and unmoved? He is in pain because, on the one hand, he is driven by his passion to destroy his unfaithful lover. But, on the other hand, he is constrained by his love and refuses to punish her.

She deserves to be punished by stoning, for the law of the land declares such punishment for those who are unfaithful after promising to marry. She has made a mockery of their betrothal by running off with another man. Their wonderful garden paradise is ruined. Weeds grow where beautiful flowers used to flourish. All their plans have been put on hold because of her unfaithfulness.

His heart is broken, but he cannot make himself destroy her. He could, though; he could wipe her off the face of the planet in an instant. He could remove her so completely that not even a memory of her would remain. But his stubborn love will not allow it. He just cannot vent his anger on the one he loves.

But he must do something. His father, the ruler of the kingdom, demands that justice be done, for he is a righteous ruler. Therefore, the jealous lover has no choice but to see his beloved die, or to die himself.

As we will see, he ends up giving up his own life to prove his love for his bride. After much thought and after suffering from deep agony in his spirit, his own death seems the only way out for both of them.

He accepts the guilt of his lover, places it on himself, and takes her punishment of death. Profound sadness fills the hearts of many who watch this horrible event unfold. What a waste! He was such a mighty man. Like a lion, he roared in the faces of his enemies, but over this wretched woman he wept like a lamb. Who was she to command such power over this man? Did it have to end like this?

However, the jealous lover has many enemies who are glad to see him die. In fact, they are not satisfied to see him stoned; instead, they subject him to the torturous death of crucifixion. They sneer with delight as they watch him suffer and die.

But is it really the end? It is true that, throughout time, death has marked the end of hope. It has killed so many dreams and has turned off all the lights on many bright futures. Too many brides-to-be have been left all alone because death claimed their men before the men could become their husbands.

But this is not a hopeless story. Death claims no victory here. The grave does not flaunt its keeping power this time. No, not even death can destroy the dream of happiness for the jealous lover, because this is the ultimate love story. And real love always finds a way.

## PRACTICAL APPLICATION

There is no greater message throughout the Scriptures than *"God is love"* (1 John 4:8). His creation, His actions, even His judgments all center on His love. His Son, Jesus, suffered a brutal death to prove just how much He loves you.

Of all that is said about God, the most intriguing statement is that God is a jealous God. (See Exodus 20:5.) The Scriptures have much to say about this attribute of God. It fascinates me that God has a jealous streak. I have studied this concept and discovered some interesting facts.

# A Jealous God

Jealousy is often linked with envy. However, the concepts of the two words are drastically different. Envy is a feeling of resentful discontent, begrudging admiration, or covetousness with regard to another's advantages, possessions, or attainments; it is a strong desire for something possessed by another. The word *envy* is always used in this sense.

Jealousy, on the other hand, is a strong, passionate desire for and guarding of one's own possessions. While the word *jealousy* can sometimes be used in the same way as *envy,* there is much more to the word than coveting another's possessions—especially when the jealous One is God, because God cannot be envious! (See 1 Corinthians 13:4, compared with the New King James Version, for instance.) Discovering this distinction was the key for me. God is not simply a creator; He is not just a custodian of His world. He has compelling emotion and enthusiasm for, love for, and interest in His people. He protects that relationship and gets furious when anything or anybody seeks to destroy the intimacy He cherishes with His people.

His feelings are much like the deep feelings a husband has for his wife. God characterizes His love that way in the Scriptures. Often He uses the husband-and-wife metaphor to explain His relationship with Israel in the Old Testament and then His relationship with the church in the New.

(See, for example, Isaiah 54:5 and 2 Corinthians 11:2.) No Bible passage speaks to this issue with more power than Exodus 34:14: *"For you shall not worship any other god, for the LORD, whose name is Jealous, is a jealous God."*

Instead of seeing these words with religious eyes, I ask you to hear these words with romantic ears. God is saying to His people, "I love you and cannot allow you to adore, reverence, and honor anyone else more than Me. I must have your absolute loyalty and exclusive devotion. Call Me Jealous, and I'll answer. Because I am jealous, I'm consumed with My love for you. I'll fight for you and be there for you. But I must have you for Myself, and I will not be satisfied until it is so." What a message this is for us!

After many years of pastoring, and after reflecting upon my own experiences with God, I am convinced that too many believers miss the real message of God's love for them. They are content with the rhetoric of His love, but the reality of that love and what it means escapes them. They are satisfied with so little of all that God has to offer.

By remaining unaware of the full measure of His love for them—through either apathy or ignorance of God's Word—they are defenseless against the psychological games played by their enemy, Satan. Recall that the betrothed was unfaithful to the jealous lover; she was captivated by the trickster and ran off with him. This is how so many people are today; they become too easily swayed by the temptations of life. They are unaware of just how passionate Christ is about His love relationship with them.

An interesting question naturally follows these observations: if there is so much love to be enjoyed, why would anyone not open himself or herself up to it? Why would anyone settle for so little?

I found the answers when I began counseling people as part of the marriage and family ministry that my wife and I conduct across the country. The problem is that too many people have no idea what love is.

Some people do not know because, during the course of their lives, they've never experienced anyone actually loving them. As strange as it may seem, there are many people who have never felt real love. This one fact alone can devastate some people. Never being touched, held, or caressed, never hearing anyone tell them how much they are needed, can ruin their view of life.

In some cases, their parents were guilty of treating them like servants instead of like the precious gifts of God that they are. Their home lives were too bad to reveal. They had to make it through life on their own. When they grew up, they scratched out a living. They were born victims, raised unwanted, and sent into the world unprotected and open for abuse. They searched for love in all the wrong places and instead found reasons for wishing they'd never been born.

Others do not know what real love is because they are convinced that it is not for them and never will be. They have absolutely no feelings of self-worth. They are lonely and depressed. They have a fatalistic view of life. They have judged themselves to be unworthy of love.

No one told them that love does not come into a person's life by merit. It is not an award or reward. True love is unconditional. Love is a profoundly tender, deeply passionate affection for another person. It is a warm, personal attachment and commitment to another person. It is a gift. This concept is foreign to them.

Consequently, whenever anyone shows any kind of affection toward them, they immediately conclude that something is wrong with the picture. They scrutinize every word and question every motive, looking for hidden meaning that will verify their suspicions. And they generally presume the worst, no matter what the evidence shows.

Then there is the group of people who know what love is, desire love, and willingly give love away. But people incapable of appreciating the gift trample on their loving nature. Abused, used, and spent, they vow never to be fooled again. They build up impressive brick walls designed to keep everybody out. They don't want to think about love, have love, or be loving because they've been hurt. They assume that, because they have known so much pain, everyone they will meet in the future will bring pain with them.

And yet, deep within the souls of all three types of people lies a hunger to know and have love. I've known people who were so desperate to find love that they physically abused themselves, hoping to prompt a loving response from someone else. Threats of self-mutilation and suicide were acceptable means to them for seeking love.

Before I became a minister, I had no idea that people were in this much pain. I also didn't realize that I, too, was suffering from a love disorder. But God revealed Himself to me with tender care and great patience. I discovered His love after a long and sometimes disturbing process.

What I've learned I will share with you. I hope to bring into better focus for you just how much God loves you and what that means for your daily walk with Him. My prayer is that the presentation of the case of the jealous lover will move you to appreciate God more and to love Him better.

# Part Two

*Chapter Five*

# *The Facts As We Know Them*

*Chapter Five*

# The Facts As
# We Know Them

*A*lone. That word seems best to describe the jealous lover during the days leading up to and including his death. Those who witnessed his death agree that he was despised and rejected, a man of sorrows, acquainted with grief. He had no advocate to plead his cause, no victim's rights committee to come to his aid.

The last days of his life were perpetually painful, and they came to a painful end. He was beaten without mercy. It's a wonder that none of his bones were broken.

## The Case of the Jealous Lover

The people of his community treated him like a freak show in a circus. There were many who took pleasure in his sufferings. They taunted him, and some even spit at him, expressing their utter contempt of his person.

He was treated as a high offender. The worst criminals were sentenced to die by crucifixion, and he was forced to carry the instrument of his own execution: a cruel cross designed to maximize his sufferings. Stripped of all his clothes, naked and past shame, he was fastened to the tree of woe.

The crisp sound of metal hitting metal as the stakes were driven into his wrists and feet should have masked his cries of pain. But it didn't, only because he made no such cry.

His silence suggested that he had accepted his fate. His voice was mute except when used to verify that he was a rejected man. He was heard asking the question: "Why have you abandoned me?"

He had known he was going to die. He and his father had agreed on the best plan of action, but it was still difficult for him to carry it through. For three hours the night before, he had pleaded with his father to make another way for the penalty to be paid, until great drops of bloody sweat poured from his body.

After pouring out his heart to his father, the jealous lover gained peace about what he would face. One can only imagine what the last moments of this poor victim's life must have been like—tortured until death became his rescue.

One of those who witnessed the jealous lover's brutal death was a local detective with an inquisitive mind. He had seen many public executions but none like this one. He had to find out the full story of the jealous lover's life and death. Why had the jealous lover agreed to take this drastic punishment upon himself? Why had his final days been so full of pain and his death so torturous? Who was behind all this? The detective would not stop until he had found the answers to these questions.

### The Scene of Death

The detective stepped forward and began to examine the scene. The authorities recognized him but left him alone, assuming he was on official business. He knew that evidence must be collected and preserved. Great care must be taken to gather as much information as possible.

The scene was a bloody mess. "It is quite unusual to have this much blood at an execution like this," the detective said to himself. He decided to send a sample to the laboratory for analysis, thinking that it would provide an intriguing case for the lab technicians.

## The Case of the Jealous Lover

The execution stake, plunged into the earth like a dagger, held the limp body of the victim. There was a strange quiet at the scene. Some people were milling around in a state of shock. But most of them had scattered, afraid that they, too, might one day suffer a similar fate. The body, still dripping blood, hung lifeless and pitiful.

The air was still and quiet, like the peace before a storm. The only sound was that of drops of blood as they splattered onto the ground. Hearing them hit with such precision forced the detective to count along as if he were numbering something.

There was so much blood; the ground was soaked with it. "The body must be almost completely drained of the life fluid," the detective theorized. Swarms of flies had gathered, called to the feast by the pungent smell of death. An eerie darkness covered the area like a shroud, almost as if trying to hide from view the horrific scene and to recover some dignity for the victim.

Even though the sky was dark, making things difficult to see, the detective could tell that the body had been mutilated. Ribbons of flesh dangled from the victim's back, and his bones had been exposed. The victim's face was unrecognizable and extremely swollen, no doubt owing to repeated blows to the head.

## The Facts As We Know Them

The detective could tell that the torturers had beaten him without mercy before killing him. They had used a whip, but not just any whip. The executioners had used the kind employed by trained torturers: a whip designed to produce maximum suffering, called the cat-o'-nine-tails. The detective had seen this whip used before. He recalled that it was usually made of nine strands of leather, each about five feet in length. Two- to three-inch pieces of bone and metal were implanted in the strands. An expert could wield this whip with great effectiveness.

The detective began to imagine how the flogger lashed out at his victim, allowing the whip to wrap around the body. Then, with a powerful flick of his wrist, the whip had been summoned back, ripping flesh as it departed. The detective knew that the pain of such torture is unbearable. He had heard that a master flogger could usher a victim to the very door of death. "If death doesn't come after a person receives such a whipping, he wishes it had," the detective thought.

The amount of damage to the jealous lover's body indicated to the detective that the forty-lash punishment had probably been used. He knew that men of might and power feared the thought of receiving forty lashes, even if they had committed no crime. This was the most severe category of flogging, reserved for the fiercest of criminals.

"What did this man do to deserve this much pain?" the detective wondered.

As the detective looked more closely, he saw that the flogging alone could not account for all the victim's wounds. There was a gaping hole in his side—not a rip or tear, but more like a slice, as if a knife blade had pierced the dead man's side.

It was obvious that the executioners had wanted to make sure this victim would not live to see the next day. As the detective pondered this, a crimson trail of blood ebbed its way down the victim's body to the earth below him. "An autopsy must be performed, but by the looks of this hole, this could very well be the cause of death," thought the detective.

"The law of the land requires that all dead bodies must be buried within twenty-four hours of the time of their death. No preservatives are used to embalm the dead here. Having him buried so quickly will complicate the investigation, but it will not hinder the discovery of evidence," the detective reasoned.

The detective learned from a bystander that a wealthy businessman, named Joseph, had allowed the victim to borrow his grave—again an unusual occurrence. It seemed to be a contradiction in terms to "borrow a grave." Would Joseph share the site with this victim, or did the victim's family plan on exhuming the body and relocating it at a later date?

## *The Autopsy*

The detective was aware that in similar cases of crucifixion, the coroner's office did not usually have to perform an autopsy to determine the cause of death. A brief examination at the scene was often sufficient. But he also knew that this case was remarkably different—so different, in fact, that the authorities did not want any surprises or any lingering questions about this execution.

Knowing that an autopsy would accompany this case, the detective contacted an old friend, the coroner. He asked the coroner if he could observe the autopsy. The coroner replied that such a favor seemed like a small thing to do for an old friend.

With the detective present as an observer, the coroner performed the jealous lover's autopsy with great interest and began to write his report. The report revealed some intriguing facts to him, some of which presented more questions than they answered. He began by writing the easy part first, while the detective looked over his shoulder.

> The victim was a male, about thirty-four years old, and generally in good physical condition.

## The Case of the Jealous Lover

> There are no signs of chemical dependency in his system. Not even the usual painkillers administered to people killed by crucifixion can be found in his blood.

The coroner stopped writing for a moment. "I must study that blood in greater detail," he said to the detective. Then he continued writing:

> There are large areas of swelling, of a kind associated with beatings. Numerous abrasions and contusions cover his body. His back is in shreds, with large sections of muscle and skin tissue almost completely separated from his bones.
>
> The distinctive puncture marks associated with this type of death have been found in both wrists and feet. Careful examination of the holes in his appendages reveals that stretching activity occurred.

The coroner knew that this type of stretching resulted from the victim's desperate attempts to shift the weight of his body from his arms to his legs and then back again. He explained the physical effects of this desperate struggle to the detective: "As his body hung, supported only by the strength of the tissues, bones, and tendons located in the metacarpal tunnel of his wrists, the muscles in his arms experienced spasms—uncontrollable shaking that produces cramplike pain. The spasms were the visible result of fatigued muscles and hypercarbia, a condition brought on by the inability to breathe out enough of the carbon dioxide in the body. All of this was made worse by the victim's dehydrated state.

"Apparently the victim had attempted to shift the burden of the weight of his body from his arm muscles to his legs. Pushing off on the stakes in his feet, he had tried to allow his legs to hold him up. But soon the muscles in his legs had started cramping, too. It was a painful death." Having explained the awful pain involved, the coroner made a note of it.

He began to examine the four-inch slice located in the victim's side. He wrote,

> The puncture wound extends into his thoracic cavity. The blade proceeded toward the heart, rupturing the pericardium, the protective membranous sac enclosing the heart.
>
> The strain on his heart was great, owing to the traumatic blood loss, fatigue, and dehydration of this tortuous death. The heart had difficulty keeping the body fluids circulating and delivering oxygen to the body. This resulted in the watery build-up of fluids around the lungs and heart.
>
> This injury accounts for the significant blood and water loss reported at the scene,

but was not the actual cause of death. This injury was sustained after his death. In fact, nothing examined so far is the sole cause of this victim's death.

The coroner noticed other things that seemed to defy explanation. His report continued:

> With all the severe physical abuse this victim suffered, there are absolutely no broken bones. Stakes were driven into his wrists and feet, but neither the carpal or metacarpal bones in the hand nor the tarsal or metatarsal bones in his feet were broken.
>
> He was beaten about the head and shoulders. His head is swollen to two times its normal size. However, the fragile bones of his face are not broken.
>
> The blade that caused the thoracic injury reached his pericardium but never injured his ribs.
>
> On his back he had to carry his execution platform, the weight of which must have been too much for him to bear. That back was beaten until his bones were exposed, but after all of that abuse, not a single vertebra was fractured.
>
> But the strangest observation of all is that this body—dead now for several hours— has shown no signs of rigor mortis. His extremities are still flexible.

# The Facts As We Know Them

The detective interrupted the coroner. "What do you make of that?" he asked.

The coroner shook his head. "I don't know. Rigor mortis is the first sign of bodily decomposition, but this body is not stiff at all. Rigor mortis hasn't occurred yet here. I've never seen this before."

With that, the coroner returned to his report:

> The time of this victim's death presents a problem in determining the cause of death. The timing of his death is inconsistent with this type of terminal event. He should have survived for at least twenty-four to forty-eight hours.
>
> He should have died from cardiac arrest or hypovolemic shock, but he didn't. There was almost total blood loss, which certainly could account for death. However, in this case, the blood loss occurred after death. It is almost as if by a deliberate decision he just expired.
>
> After performing this autopsy, it is the opinion of the coroner that this office cannot declare conclusively exactly what the cause of death was in this case.

The coroner concluded that the cause of death was psychological or emotional rather than physical. The detective took a deep breath and said, "So the question remains: What really caused the death of this man?"

## *Still Determined*

The detective returned to his office and reread the autopsy report, looking for evidence he might have overlooked. Then, in a fit of frustration, he slammed the report on his desk. "I was hoping for more clues than this," he said aloud, though he was talking to himself. "I need answers, not more questions. Somebody was behind this man's torturous death, and I don't care if I have to study his whole life—I will find out what really happened here!"

An associate, overhearing his outcries and hoping to ease his burden by being his sounding board, asked him about his progress.

The detective told his colleague, "I've gone over the place of execution thoroughly. I was counting on the autopsy report to solve part of the puzzle, but it came back inconclusive. I've interviewed everyone directly associated with his execution, but still I'm stuck.

"Because it was such a violent death, I suspect that someone tried to get him out of the way. Whoever was responsible for this didn't just want him dead; they also wanted him to suffer.

"I know that he died, I know when he died, but I don't know what caused his death or who was behind it. I'm stuck and don't know where to go from here."

The associate quite innocently said, "Wait a second. Isn't it obvious that the executioners were behind all this?"

"That's exactly my dilemma," said the detective. "The executioners killed the jealous lover, but someone manipulated this situation for his own devilish purposes. There's more to this case than just the obvious."

"Why don't you start from the beginning?" the associate suggested. "Build a profile of the jealous lover's life."

The detective got his coat and left the building. He began an in-depth search for information and was still looking for answers on the third day after the jealous lover's death. After pursuing several leads with little success, he went to the gravesite of the victim in order to think and to try to find more clues. This was the strangest case he had ever investigated. There are so many missing pieces of this puzzle.

The victim was stabbed after he died, and none of his wounds caused his death. He was entombed in a borrowed grave—a borrowed grave? "This is so mysterious," the detective thought. Then, as he looked at the gravesite, he said, "If you could only talk to me, what would you say? I've got to know who...."

The detective's words were broken off by a touch on his shoulder. He turned to see a man whose gentle hand was still resting on him.

"Who are you?" the detective asked.

The man answered that he was the victim's father. "You're just the man I want to see," said the detective, who was thinking, "This may be the break I've been hoping for. Surely the father must know something." Overwhelmed by this turn of events, the detective tried to regain his composure. He knew that a case like this one could take years or decades to solve.

"I'm sorry that you had to see your son die as he did," the detective told the victim's father, who was nodding his head to acknowledge the detective's condolences. "But I promise you, sir, I will get to the bottom of this unfortunate event and see that justice is served. Now, let me ask you...."

The father lifted his hand to prevent the steady stream of questions he knew the detective would ask. "Young man, I know you are filled with questions. Let me assure you that I do have the answers you seek. And before this case is solved, the death of my son will not be the only significant thing you'll remember about this. But for now, I'll just remind you of the name that describes my son's personality: the jealous lover. Let me tell you about him by reading from his journal."

The two of them sat down beside the grave and made themselves comfortable. From the sound of it, the detective knew that this was going to be a story he had to hear.

*Chapter Six*

## *"Meet Me Tonight"*

*Chapter Six*

# *"Meet Me Tonight"*

*The LORD did not set His love on you nor choose you
because you were more in number than any of the
peoples, for you were the fewest of all peoples,
but because the LORD loved you.
—Deuteronomy 7:7–8*

*The cool of the evening is our time together.
We meet at our favorite place in the world.
At dusk, when the sun casts a gentle amber
glow in the sky, my lover and I rush to the place of
our rendezvous. I look forward to these moments
we share.*

*I live for the moment when I see that smile
light up her face. When she hears the sound of my*

*footsteps, she turns around to see me and just glows.*

*She never knows exactly when I am coming; her wondering if I will be there every night keeps the mystery in the relationship alive.*

*When I first began to spend time with her, I didn't bring flowers. Instead, I planted gardens. I created a floral tribute to our love. I filled the gardens with all kinds of beautiful plants that bloomed constantly. I strategically placed stately trees throughout this paradise I created.*

*Little streams of water course their way through the gardens. The babbling of the water is so relaxing.*

*These flowering gardens have become our special meeting place. Gentle breezes, blowing the fragrance of the evening roses, set the mood. We often talk for hours, communicating our love to each other under the stars while watching the moon walk across the night sky.*

*Everything is perfect. I love every minute of it, because this is real. She is special to me.*

*I have power; I have servants who work for me, but they are under my control. She came to me willingly, eagerly. I also have much wealth, but my lover loves me for who I am. We are connected by an unseen power. I want things to stay like this forever.*

## "Meet Me Tonight"

*The sound of her voice is like poetry to my ears. We often talk about life in general. She tells me all kinds of things. It doesn't all make sense, but I don't mind. I want to hear all of it because everything that matters to her matters to me.*

*Now, she always worries about little things that I have already taken care of. I have to reassure her constantly that I am in total control.*

*The truth is, I can read her mind. By the time she asks for most things, they are already done.*

*Some things, however, I will not do for her until she asks me to do them. I do this just because it thrills me to hear her ask me to take care of something. Now that it has been a while, she has started trusting me enough to presume that I will take care of everything.*

*I know you are wondering, "Who is this love of your life, and how did you find her? She sounds so special when you talk about her." Indeed, she is special.*

*The strange thing is that she was not special before I found her. She didn't come from a prestigious family. Actually, she was unwanted even by her own mother. Abandoned and left to die, she had no future and no hope. I still do not know who her father is.*

*But when I saw her, something jumped in my heart. I fell in love with her and decided that she must be mine. I think about her all the time. All day, I think about her. All night long, I think about her. I love this woman.*

## PRACTICAL APPLICATION

When you love someone, you want to spend as much time as possible with him or her. Love often begins when a total stranger catches your eye. You become fascinated with that person. You see him or her, and you lose your sense of calm. You want to get close to, talk to, and be with that person. If you know someone who knows this new love interest of yours, you try to use your influence to have your friend introduce the two of you.

Friends close to you notice that you have a love interest. They start making inquiries. "Who is this person?" they ask. "What is he like?" The list goes on and on. Sometimes those same friends get a bit envious of you because you don't spend as much time with them as you used to. There is a new person in your life who consumes your interest. You try to explain your situation to your friends, but they do not understand.

You are in love. You are interested in learning everything there is to know about this person. How he or she reacts to situations and your questions shapes how you approach that person. When you know you've found someone special, it doesn't take long to start thinking about the future.

In the early stages of a love relationship, you want to please the other person. Under no circumstances must anything go wrong with this relationship. You feel a need to impress upon that person that you are the one for him or her. You do not want him or her to leave before finding out that the two of you are soul mates.

The process of developing a relationship with another person has stayed the same throughout the ages. There are two essential procedures that make a relationship work: spending quality time together and communicating with one another. These activities are the backbone of love relationships. This is not too difficult for us to understand when we observe a relationship between two people. However, it is very hard for many people to view their relationship with God in this light.

The reason for this is that God is not just another person. We respect, even revere, His omnipotence, His omniscience, and His omnipresence. In other words, we recognize that He is all-powerful, all-knowing, and everywhere at once. It is important for us to know these qualities and to honor Him for them. However, concentrating on these divine attributes alone may cause us to miss a precious part of who God is.

## The Case of the Jealous Lover

Our God is a person with feelings and desires. He does not want to be ignored, abused, or mistreated. He is love, He gives love, and He wants love in return. He gets offended whenever He is approached like a resource when He is needed, and then dismissed by us when the crisis is over. He wants to mean something to us because of who He is. He does not want us to come to Him only because of what He can do for us.

Do you remember how happy the jealous lover is because his beloved is in love with him for who he is? This is exactly what God wants from His people.

Many people who are unfamiliar with God have a flawed view of Him. They think of God only in philosophical terms. Because people are generally not interested in getting to know the Lord as He is, they substitute their own ideas about Him for the truth. Their thoughts about God are a mixture of human inventions.

God is often referred to by these people as The Man Upstairs, The Force, and a host of other titles. These terms characterize God as a distant entity that hovers over creation, performing necessary maintenance tasks for the earth. To a large degree, many people feel that God is unknowable. This understanding of God frees them from any commitment to Him personally. To them, He is unapproachable.

Many well-meaning believers have a confused definition of God, as well. They think of God in religious ways. That is, they know Him through church doctrine and church services, but their relationship to Him is hindered by their religion—by their overemphasis on knowledge and works. As a result, it is easy for them to quote Scripture about God and to talk about Him, but they have no intimacy with Him.

They have accepted Christ as Savior and Lord, but they discuss Him using official "church terms." For example, they are eager to speak about His almighty power and His glory, but they do so from an emotional distance. Too many believers are willing to pursue God purely in an academic fashion. They just do not have a real, ongoing relationship with Him. It is this perspective that makes it difficult for people to pray to Him.

### Prayer as Communication

Prayer is an intimate form of communication, one of the two necessary components of a successful relationship. But how do you pray to an abstract idea or philosophy? To do so would make a person feel a bit silly. If we see someone talking to himself in a room, we think that he is somewhat strange. If we are bold enough, we inquire, "To whom are you talking?" In the same way, people feel uncomfortable talking to the air.

This is the point: God is not the air or a force or a concept or a philosophy. He is a person. You can talk to Him and hear from Him. You can appeal to Him and be touched by Him. He is real, and He wants to share many things with you. He wants to have an ongoing dialogue with you.

The word *dialogue* denotes more than merely talking. If you were to talk to yourself, it would be a monologue or soliloquy. Prayer is not making a speech; it is having a conversation with the Father.

The Lord never intended for prayer to be a task you are obligated to perform. It is not supposed to be an assignment. He did not intend prayer to be a prerequisite for remaining in good standing with your local church. The Father did not expect prayer to be a display of your preaching skills. It is neither a performance nor a demonstration of your spirituality. People who covet the reputation of being a prayer warrior miss the point.

It is not important that other people know you pray frequently; it is important that the Father hears from you frequently. Praying is not supposed to be an asset you list on your résumé. Prayer is an expression of your love for the Lord. Remember, when you share love with someone, you want to spend time with and talk to him or her. You look forward to sharing your secrets and accomplishments because you know he or she is interested. You are not embarrassed to tell your hurts and pains and disappointments because you know the other person will understand.

### Prayer as Shared Love

Understanding prayer to be communication alone is not sufficient. Even recognizing that prayer is supposed to be a dialogue—a two-way discussion—is not enough, either. You must cherish prayer as one of your most effective means of sharing your love with the Father.

Consider the people in the Bible who were known to be close to God. Thank God He allowed us to eavesdrop on their conversations with Him! When you read their prayers and the Lord's responses, you do not get the feeling that they were having a board meeting or sales seminar. There was love going on. People like David and Paul and others talked to God and heard from God. It was wonderful. Let's take a look into their prayer lives.

### David's Thirst for God

You can almost feel David's love for God when you read, *"As the deer pants for the water brooks,*

*so my soul pants for Thee, O God"* (Psalm 42:1).
Oh, you can sense the passion! This was not a casual reference to God. David said, "My desire for
God is like the need a deer has for water. When a
deer is thirsty, nothing else matters until the
thirst is satisfied." Essentially, David was saying,
"Lord I'm panting after You. I will not rest until
I am satisfied. My adrenaline is active; my
breathing is rapid; my excitement level is high. I
anticipate our rendezvous. I must meet with
You!"

In Psalm 63, David again expressed his longing for God:

*O God, my God! How I search for you! How I
thirst for you in this parched and weary land
where there is no water. How I long to find
you! How I wish I could go into your sanctu-
ary to see your strength and glory, for your
love and kindness are better to me than life it-
self. How I praise you! I will bless you as long
as I live, lifting up my hands to you in prayer.
At last I shall be fully satisfied; I will praise
you with great joy. I lie awake at night thinking of you—of how much you have helped
me—and how I rejoice through the night beneath the protecting shadow of your wings. I
follow close behind you, protected by your
strong right arm.        (Psalm 63:1–8 TLB)*

# "Meet Me Tonight"

Read these words of David's conversation with God. What deep desire he had for the presence of the Lord! These are the kind of heartfelt words that move God to act. Can you not imagine God, after hearing this kind of prayer, saying, "Whatever you need, David, I am going to get for you"?

God answers this type of prayer. His response to our heartfelt longing for Him is exemplified by His words in Isaiah 49:

> *Can a woman forget her nursing child, and have no compassion on the son of her womb? Even these may forget, but I will not forget you. Behold, I have inscribed you on the palms of My hands; your walls are continually before Me.* (Isaiah 49:15–16)

What reassurance the Lord offers! "I am not going to forget you, ever," He says. The best part of this passage is the first part of verse sixteen: *"Behold, I have inscribed you on the palms of My hands."*

With these words, the Lord seeks to demonstrate just how certain He is that He will not forget us. He declares that He has engraved us on the palms of His hands. What an image!

The word *engrave* means "to cut as in stone, to chisel into; to scratch into." The Lord says to each of us, "I am going to ensure that I will remember you. In My hands I have chiseled your name. When I lift My hands, your name will ever be before My eyes." This is the sort of thing that someone in love would do.

How many young men do you know who have written a lover's name on their hands or carved the name on their possessions? God says, "I have scratched your name in My hand."

In Psalm 63, David told the Lord that he stayed awake at night thinking about Him. Then, in Psalm 139, David told God how comforted he was to discover that the Lord was thinking about him, not just at night, but all the time:

> *How precious it is, Lord, to realize that you are thinking about me constantly! I can't even count how many times a day your thoughts turn toward me. And when I waken in the morning, you are still thinking of me!*
> *(Psalm 139:17–18 TLB)*

When David had long since fallen asleep at night, God was still thinking about him. When David woke up the next morning, the Lord was still thinking about him. When David tried to count the number of God's thoughts toward him, he got tired of counting before he ran out of thoughts to count.

## "Meet Me Tonight"

This is how you talk when you're in love with someone. You cannot force this or produce this kind of conversation out of obligation. This kind of interchange can only occur in an intimate relationship.

### Paul's Desire to Understand God

The apostle Paul knew how to talk to God as well. Communication with God came easily to Paul because he was totally devoted to the Lord. His passion for God was so intense that he even chose not to marry. (See 1 Corinthians 7:7–8, 32–33.) He was overwhelmed by his feelings toward his God. He wanted all that God had to offer and more.

Paul had a "death wish." It was not, however, a wish to escape from life, but a desire to be with the Lord whom he loved.

> *For to me, to live is Christ, and to die is gain. But if I am to live on in the flesh, this will mean fruitful labor for me; and I do not know which to choose. But I am hard-pressed from both directions, having the desire to depart and be with Christ, for that is very much better; yet to remain on in the flesh is more necessary for your sake.* *(Philippians 1:21–24)*

Paul didn't spend much time asking God for life-sustaining blessings. Instead, he sought to know the Lord. Read some of his expressions in Philippians 3:

> *But whatever things were gain to me, those things I have counted as loss for the sake of Christ. More than that, I count all things to be loss in view of the surpassing value of knowing Christ Jesus my Lord, for whom I have suffered the loss of all things, and count them but rubbish in order that I may gain Christ, and may be found in Him, not having a righteousness of my own derived from the Law, but that which is through faith in Christ, the righteousness which comes from God on the basis of faith, that I may know Him, and the power of His resurrection and the fellowship of His sufferings, being conformed to His death; in order that I may attain to the resurrection from the dead. Not that I have already obtained it, or have already become perfect, but I press on in order that I may lay hold of that for which also I was laid hold of by Christ Jesus.*                                      *(Philippians 3:7–12)*

It is obvious here that Paul loved the Lord. He devalued every other aspect of his life when it was compared with his Lord. The New American Standard translation uses the word *"rubbish"* in verse eight, but the King James Version uses the word *"dung."* *"Dung"* is the better word. In Paul's view, there was no value to all the things that he had accomplished outside of the Lord. They were worth nothing more than dung to him.

In this passage, Paul expressed his desire to know every aspect of the Lord. He wanted to know His triumphs, His sufferings, even His death. In essence, Paul wanted the Lord to know that he was going to follow Him all the time. He was not only interested in the good times; he wanted every experience he could have with the Lord.

God took Paul to the third heaven, to a place Paul referred to as paradise. There God showed him things that Paul reported he was not permitted to reveal. (See 2 Corinthians 12:2–4.) Of course, the fact that he could not tell us makes us want to know all the more. But to know more, you have to get close to the Lord yourself.

### The Disciples' Walk of Faith

Peter and John, two disciples of Jesus Christ, also had intimate relationships with the Lord that were characterized by meaningful communication. It was clear by their lives that they had *"been with Jesus"* (Acts 4:13). Let me describe an incident in their lives that illustrates this.

Christ had recently ascended to heaven while all the disciples watched. He had left them with the responsibility of representing Him on earth. They took their assignment seriously; they immediately started witnessing for Christ, making disciples and performing miracles. (See Mark 16:14–20.)

Their actions and their message were radical. They were not received well by the prevailing religious powers of that day. But the common people to whom the disciples spoke embraced them and received the message of God's grace with enthusiasm. This vigorous reception of the gospel message infuriated the Pharisees and Sadducees, who had hoped that they were done with Christ at His death. This "Christ problem" just would not go away.

A most notable miracle was performed right outside the Pharisees' and Sadducees' "front door." Just outside the temple gate, Peter and John healed a man who had been lame since birth (Acts 3:1–8). The Pharisees and Sadducees learned of the miracle and were disturbed that Peter and John were preaching the resurrection of Christ (Acts 4:1–2.) They were determined to stop the disciples by persecuting them and putting them on trial. When they went to do so, they stumbled because the miracles Peter and John had performed were so well-known. Even using devious means, the Pharisees and Sadducees found it difficult to persecute these men because their works approved them before the people. This was unsettling for the Pharisees and Sadducees.

Peter and John were not lettered in theology. They had not been educated in a prep school for the gifted and talented. They were ordinary men who had been given an extraordinary opportunity to work for the Lord.

The example of Peter and John is different from those of David and Paul because their own testimony about their relationship with God is not recorded. But in this incident, their enemies testified about their relationship with the Lord.

Almost all the important leaders of the Jewish religion participated in the trial of Peter and John. They were worried about allowing someone to operate in ministry who didn't have their approval. They wanted to know whose authority gave Peter and John the permission to preach and teach. The disciples knew that this was their hour in which to glorify God. They were ready with an answer.

What gives this story such meaning? I don't think it was their rebuttal speech or their emotional style of delivery. It wasn't even the courageous faith they displayed by standing up to that corrupt court and speaking out on behalf of Christ. The power of this story can be seen in the reaction of the Pharisees and Sadducees to the lives of Peter and John.

The Pharisees took note of the religious background of the disciples and judged them to be unqualified to represent God in the earth. According to the Pharisees and Sadducees, one had to attain a certain level of education before he could be qualified to speak for God. Peter and John were not qualified—they were *"unlearned and ignorant men"* (Acts 4:13 KJV). They were common men in the eyes of the religious community. But there was one thing about these disciples that even the most hardened religious leader had to admit: these men had *"been with Jesus"* (verse 13).

Most of the Pharisees and Sadducees were ungodly men. They did not have spiritual discernment. They were not in contact with God. Their acknowledgement that Peter and John had been with Jesus was not a consequence of their spiritual gifts. This was not a divine revelation to them. They were able to tell just what the disciples stood for by observation. When the Pharisees and Sadducees stopped long enough to look at the disciples, they could come to only one conclusion about them: these men had been with the Master.

If people were to examine your life, what conclusions would they draw? If they didn't know your church background and had never seen you go to church, would they suspect that you did? It is not always our testimonies or our public prayers that display our intimacy with God. Carrying a big Bible doesn't necessarily mean you know the Word. Writing the name of Jesus in the dust on boxes at work won't prove that you love Jesus. You cannot stumble into intimacy with the Father overnight. A real relationship with the Lord only comes from spending quality time with Him.

Don't be afraid to break out of your religious mold. Try talking to the Father like you would talk to a best friend. Tell Him everything; He can keep a secret, and He loves you. Tell Him the little things and the big things. Then listen for His voice. Don't delay; meet Him today.

## A PRAYER

*Dear Father, I pray for the person reading this book. I pray that he may know You not only as an awesome God, but also as the tender and gentle Lover of his soul.*

*Lord, let him learn just how close he can get to You. Reveal to him that You are as near to him as his mouth and his heart. (See Romans 10:8–9.) Teach him that prayer is not a performance but a time of fellowship with You. In the gardens of his prayers, walk with him. In Jesus' name, I pray. Amen.*

*Chapter Seven*

# "I Will Ask Her Tonight"

*Chapter Seven*

# "I Will Ask Her Tonight"

*"For I know the plans that I have for you,"*
*declares the LORD, "plans for welfare and not*
*for calamity to give you a future and a hope."*
*—Jeremiah 29:11*

*I*t is difficult waiting for the day to end and the evening to come. I have to ask her to be my bride. All I can think about is being with her. I think about her all night and all day. I know it sounds as if I'm repeating myself, but I love her. I love her more than she loves me.

## The Case of the Jealous Lover

*She said she loves me, too, and that my love is sweeter than wine. She enjoys telling people about me. She can't tell them too much, however, because I haven't told her everything about myself. Since our first meeting, I have only let her know so much, but she will find out everything on our wedding night. It is better this way. I haven't revealed everything to her even though she constantly asks me to. I haven't told her everything, because I want her to love me for who I am, not for what I can do for her.*

*I always meet her in the evening. People have started to notice our relationship and have asked questions. They want to know my identity.*

*Her neighbors are curious and cruel. They have talked to me about her behind her back. They can't figure out what I see in her. They call her ugly and unappealing. Her own brothers make her work in the fields. They feel justified in doing this to her because they are sure nobody really wants her. But I want her.*

*People also continue to ask her about me. She tells them about me to the best of her ability. But she doesn't know exactly who I am.*

*I know what it is like to have someone around who only wants to be with me for selfish reasons, who only wants the things I can do for her. That kind of attention is irritating to me. I am tired of feeling as though I am being used.*

## "I Will Ask Her Tonight"

I want this woman, my true love, to know that I am more than what I can do. I never want anyone to come to me only when he or she needs something. I want someone to love me whether I do anything or not. It has taken her a while, but she is beginning to understand.

It is difficult living incognito, not revealing my true self while I am around her. Many times I want to tell her who I am, but I can't. To tell her would spoil my plans. Instead, I always go to her home just as if I am a neighborhood suitor. She has no idea that I am making preparations to marry her.

Before I go to meet her, I take off my special clothes and put on common attire. When I meet her every night, I watch as her face shines, and it reminds me of a lightning bolt illuminating the evening sky. She tells me that she lives for the moments we spend together.

The time we spend together is good for her. She can escape from the stressful life she endures. She is almost friendless because she doesn't fit in anywhere. The other young ladies in the town don't like her and refuse to be with her. But they keep prying into her affairs, only to find more ways to humiliate her. This has almost destroyed her confidence.

For a long time, she lived without anyone special in her life. The mischief of the young ladies' antics hadn't helped. They had enjoyed prancing *past her house with their boyfriends on their arms, glancing over at her and smiling as if to say, "I've got a man; why don't you?" She once told me that watching them parade themselves before her and hearing them tease her had been the worst parts of her loneliness.*

*Before I came into her life, every day she would fight off depression and the feeling that she was a mistake. It didn't help her to know that her mother had abandoned her at birth. Her mother had left the child lying in a pool of blood. It's a wonder my beloved has any positive feelings about herself.*

*It is that very vulnerability that drew me to her. I saw her when everyone else overlooked her. There was something in her that was so precious to me.*

*All she really wants is for someone to love her and care for her. She wants to feel special to somebody; she wants to matter, to make a difference in someone's life.*

\* \* \*

*Well, the day finally ended, and late tonight, I went to her house to ask her to be my wife—to give her the fullness of my love and to let her know how truly special she is to me.*

*People were peeking through their windows, hoping to catch a glimpse of me, her lover. I first* told her that the time had come for me to leave temporarily. All I said to her was that I was going away on business. She tried to act bravely after I broke the news to her, but she was so nervous. She asked me all kinds of questions. When am I coming back? How will she know I am coming? Will there be a sign to alert her of my return?

I watched her as the wheels in her pretty little head started spinning. She was deep in thought.

Maybe she felt that I was going to leave her and that the prophecies of her so-called friends would come true. "You can't keep a man," they have told her every chance they have gotten.

She doesn't know where I live. So, if I left and stayed away too long, how would she find me? Her spirits fell.

I held her close to me and whispered to her that I would never forsake her. We would always be together, even to the end of time. I asked her to trust me and believe in me. Still she wanted a sign, something to hold on to, something to rest her faith upon.

I told her she didn't need a sign, but if she had to have one, it would be this: the only sign she needed to prove that I was coming back was that I had left. For as surely as I left, I would return. That I loved her and would be returning for her was all she needed to hold on to.

# The Case of the Jealous Lover

*Of course, the mystery of all this troubled her, but it will be a blessing to her later on. I am working on a surprise for her. What she doesn't know is that after our first meeting, I had gone back home and told my father about her.*

*As is our custom, I had to get his permission to marry her. My father has supervised the whole process. After I told him that I had found someone and that I wanted to spend the rest of my life with her, he gave me detailed instructions on how to proceed.*

*Part of asking her to marry me was to offer her a glass of wine. If she drank the wine, it would be a signal that she accepted my proposal. Let me tell you what happened in more detail.*

*After I told her that I would never forsake her, I asked her to marry me. Then I slowly poured a glass of my best wine, picked it up, and offered it to her. She was so excited she could hardly contain herself. She looked at the glass of wine and then at me. She looked at me and then at the glass of wine.*

*She took so long to answer, I wanted to shout at her, "Drink the wine!" But I couldn't, because she would have to make the decision freely.*

*Then she spoke, saying, "Are you sure?"*

*"Yes, I'm sure! I made my decision long ago. Drink the wine," I replied.*

*She took the glass, looked down into the crimson pool, and then drank every bit of it.*

## "I Will Ask Her Tonight"

*That was it; she had accepted my proposal. I could hardly wait to let my father know her decision. Before I left, I wanted to clarify a few things. I gently took her by her arms and told her that as surely as I lived, I would return for her. I made sure she knew my return would be a surprise and the date a secret. She must be ready at all times, because any day, even the very next day, could be when I will return for her.*

*I want her to wait for me in the meantime and think about what we are going to share together. From now on, I told her, I would think about her and talk about her as my bride.*

*I gave her this promise: "My bride, your eyes have never seen, your ears have never heard, in your wildest imaginations you've never thought about the things I am going to do for you. You think you know me, but when I come back, I am going to show you a side of me that will sweep you off your feet."*

*Then I turned and slipped into the night, leaving her with these words: "Wait for me; I will be back."*

### PRACTICAL APPLICATION

The Lord made plans for your life in eternity past. I remember the day I discovered this fact. It changed my view of God forever. Learning more about His sovereign care settled so many issues for me. It removed the fear I had about the future. It strengthened my faith.

The sovereignty of God can be explained or defined with a simple phrase: "God is in control." For years, I was taught a doctrine that unintentionally denied the sovereignty of God. If you had asked the ones who taught me their doctrine, "Do you believe in God's sovereignty?" they would have answered, "Yes!" Their teaching, however, proved that they didn't believe in it.

Their concept of His sovereignty was that God was available to help us, that He did have a plan, but that His plan could be nullified, modified, and was dependent upon circumstances.

They believed that the responsibility for my future rested upon my shoulders. What I understood from their teaching was that if I worked hard enough, was careful enough, and was spiritually "lucky," I would enjoy God's blessings and receive His help.

This was not good news! I already knew how deficient I was. Now I had to worry about trying to be perfect enough to merit God's help. Paul was correct: I was indeed a *"wretched man"* (Romans 7:24).

## "I Will Ask Her Tonight"

Then the Lord sent someone to me, in much the same way as He sent Aquila and Priscilla to Apollos, to show me *"the way of God more perfectly"* (Acts 18:26 KJV). I was astonished to learn that God was responsible for both the grand design and the minute details of my life.

Remember that His saving you did not depend upon your approval, just your acceptance. Actually, your acceptance of Him was in His plan. It is amazing how much thought went into His diagram of your life. His love for you is not infatuation. That is, He didn't just see you and decide on the spot to get involved with you. He knew you *"before the foundation of the world"* (Ephesians 1:4). He has plans for you.

The book of Jeremiah contributes to our understanding of this by teaching us that the thoughts of God toward us are not for evil, but good: *"'For I know the plans that I have for you,' declares the LORD, 'plans for welfare and not for calamity to give you a future and a hope'"* (Jeremiah 29:11). It is important to understand that the ultimate outcome of the life of the believer is set. Jeremiah stated that God's thoughts for us are to bring us to a predetermined end.

Now, this is good news. Just knowing that someone is dedicated to your success is a blessing. So often people live for weeks and months without anyone telling them, "I was thinking about you." When you get a note, a bouquet of flowers, a box of candy, or a phone call unexpectedly, your heart is immediately uplifted. But when you know that God is dedicated to your success, you can rejoice that the love of God is much more intricate than mere consideration.

God's love is intense and extremely powerful, going well beyond the ordinary. He loved us enough to prepare in advance for everything that would affect us. Our physical well-being, emotional stability, and mental health are His concerns, and providing solutions to our problems is His delight. He wants to bring peace to our lives.

The love He has for us is a bit of heaven on earth. If you see Him as merely a benevolent caretaker, you miss the best that He offers. Yes, He cares about your concerns, your hurts, your pains, and your other discomforts. Yes, He will vigorously defend you against all enemies. But His plan for your life goes much further than restoring you to a peaceful state. He wants you to thrive, not just survive.

Too many people settle for just making it through the difficulties that come along, when they could be living lives of peace. They are happy if they can hold their heads above the waters of trouble. Essentially, they are leaving God out of the picture, when God is the One who has drawn the picture.

In Ephesians 3:20, Paul spoke about the readiness of God to work on our behalf when trouble and difficulty come our way. He wrote, *"Now to Him who is able to do exceeding abundantly beyond all that we ask or think, according to the power that works within us."* Paul said that the Lord is not only going to meet our needs, He is also going to exceed them with power and love to spare.

### God's Plans for You

The Lord, the Lover of your soul, has a plan for your life that has accounted for every aspect of your need for salvation. His plan includes your deliverance, your peace, and your future glorification in heaven. He is not interested in just rescuing you from the effects of sin and preserving you from spiritual death. He wants to thrill you, elevate you, and live within you. Then He wants to glorify you in your resurrected body.

I want to discuss this part of God's plan for us in some detail. Many believers are ignorant of the promise of glorification. They are schooled in various aspects of salvation. They have quite a few definitions of sanctification. They understand duty and responsibility. The Rapture is a concept they can understand well enough. But they spend little time on glorification. Too many believers know how to covet the best spiritual gifts (1 Corinthians 12:31), and they are eager to do greater works than Christ did (John 14:12), but they never stop to consider that their salvation package includes their glorification.

It is rare to hear preachers preach on the glory reserved for the believer, but the doctrine of glorification is precious, too. It is a wonderful expression of the love of God. In John 17:5, Jesus prayed to the Father, *"Glorify Thou Me...with the glory which I had with Thee before the world was."* Let us enjoy a precious truth in the context of this verse, because *"as He is, so also are we in this world"* (1 John 4:17). The verse seems to suggest that Jesus was aware that, in God's mind, in eternity past, He saw Jesus Christ glorified. He planned not only the sufferings of Christ, but also the glory that would follow those sufferings (1 Peter 1:11). In the same way that Jesus prayed, *"Glorify Thou Me"* (John 17:5), we ought to look toward our glorification. Remember, it's part of God's plan.

There may be times in your life when you feel as though the Lord has left you. In reality, these are the times when He is preparing to bring you to a higher level in Him. Yes, His plans include a season in your life when He seems to depart, just as the jealous lover departed from his bride. But God is there, though you cannot feel Him or sense His presence. You may not hear His voice on a daily basis, but in this season of waiting, He wants you to trust Him and have faith in Him. Your having faith is part of His plan.

When the jealous lover offered his bride a glass of his best wine, and she drank it all, he knew that she had accepted his proposal of marriage. He knew that his beloved trusted him. Have you drunk deeply from the glass that Jesus Christ has offered you? Have you accepted the wine of His Holy Spirit?

As the jealous lover assured his bride that he would never abandon her, the Lord has promised never to abandon you (Hebrews 13:5). He has promised that He will come back for you (John 14:3). Romans 8:25 says, *"But if we hope for what we do not see, with perseverance we wait eagerly for it."* Since we know that Christ keeps His promises, we can wait for Him with confidence and eagerness.

God not only promises never to abandon us, but He also redeemed and delivered us while we were in an abandoned state due to our sin and rebellion against Him. In our dramatic story, the bride of the jealous lover had been abandoned by her mother and left to die. This is exactly how

## The Case of the Jealous Lover

God viewed Israel, His chosen people, in the Old Testament:

> *As for your birth, on the day you were born your navel cord was not cut, nor were you washed with water for cleansing; you were not rubbed with salt or even wrapped in cloths. No eye looked with pity on you to do any of these things for you, to have compassion on you. Rather you were thrown out into the open field, for you were abhorred on the day you were born. When I passed by you and saw you squirming in your blood, I said to you while you were in your blood, "Live!"*
>
> *(Ezekiel 16:4–6)*

In the same way, Christ says to each of us, "Live!"

Remember, the plans that God has for you include your deliverance, your peace, and your glorification. The jealous lover knew the plans that he had for his bride; it was her faith that would bring her to the fulfillment of those plans. Do you have faith that God will bring you to a higher level in Him and that you will be glorified in heaven?

Have faith in God's Word. The Bible states that *"faith is the assurance of things hoped for, the conviction of things not seen"* (Hebrews 11:1), and it is. It is also a steadfast and unmovable confidence in

God's power to perform. Let me paraphrase the last half of Numbers 23:19, which says, *"Has He said, and will He not do it? Or has He spoken, and will He not make it good?"* My paraphrase is this: If God said He will, He will do what He said. If He spoke the promise, He will perform it. If His word was word enough to create all that exists, His word is word enough for you to rely on.

Finally, the jealous lover told his bride that she must be ready for his return at all times. Likewise, we must be ready at all times for the Lord's return. The Bible says it is the wicked person who believes that the Lord is delaying His return. This wicked man foolishly presumes that the delayed return of the Lord, if indeed it is a delay, signals his license to live in rebellion against God. (See 2 Peter 3:3–4.) He is deceived. Habakkuk 2:3 says,

> *For the vision is yet for the appointed time; it hastens toward the goal, and it will not fail. Though it tarries, wait for it; for it will certainly come, it will not delay.*

Let me borrow the words of a song: "Believe the report of the Lord, for you have an expected end and an appointed time." Indeed, the Lord has plans for you—both for your life on earth and for all eternity.

*The Case of the Jealous Lover*

## A PRAYER

*Dear Lord, I pray for my reader. Let him remember the wonderful words You whispered in his ear when You saved him. You promised that You would be there for him at all times. You also promised that You would come again for him.*

*Lord, don't let Your beloved lose heart and faint in his mind. Remind him, Lord, that You are coming and will bring his glorification with You. And remind him that he will be changed into the image of Christ "from glory to glory" (2 Corinthians 3:18). In Jesus' name, Amen.*

*Chapter Eight*

## "I Have a Surprise"

*Chapter Eight*

# *"I Have a Surprise"*

*As it is written: "Eye has not seen, nor ear heard, nor have entered into the heart of man the things which God has prepared for those who love Him."*
*—1 Corinthians 2:9 NKJV*

I watched my beloved take that cup and drink, and I became the happiest person alive. She has accepted my love for her. Now that her precious heart has accepted my token of love, even though we are not yet married, it is just as if we were.

I made sure she understands that she is unavailable to anyone else. She has to know with no hint of doubt that I am a jealous lover. I made sure *she knows that she is to follow no other. I told her in a positive way, but firmly enough to make the point, that she must remain faithful to me.*

*She asked me again how long it will be before I come back. I smiled and told her it is a secret. She started to cry. I looked at her and said, "You may cry tonight, but joy is coming tomorrow." I know she didn't understand, but those words will have to do.*

*I rushed back to my father to share my moment with him. After we spent time talking about this new development in my life, he started helping me to get ready for my bride. He gave me explicit instructions for preparing a place for my bride.*

*He refuses to allow us to marry until our home is completed, even though he has already given me permission to propose. And the home will have to pass his inspection. I started immediately to fulfill his assignment. "The mansion must be ready before you can go and get her," he told me.*

*My father is unyielding when it comes to being and doing the best. I love my father, and I am always perfectly obedient to him so that I may please him. Through him I have learned the value of an intimate relationship, because he and I are so close to each other.*

*I have to build a place well suited for my beloved. And because she has to wait for me, I want the wait to be worth it. I am so excited about what I* am preparing for her. The best part is that I know she is almost completely in the dark about my plans.

Yes, she knows that, as her intended, I am supposed to make provisions for her. But because she doesn't really know my identity, and because I haven't shown her my wealth, she is probably thinking that we will have to stay with my father for a while. Is she in for a surprise!

I walk around these days with a smile on my face as I anticipate her response. What will she do when she sees the place? Will she collapse, overwhelmed by the splendor of her new home? Will she run and jump into my arms? Or will she try to remain calm and plan a surprise of her own? Oh, the anticipation makes it difficult to wait, but I will let patience have its perfect work.

Money is no object. Some men have to build a marriage chamber as an addition to their fathers' homes because of meager finances. But my father is rich, and he loves his only son. Whatever I want or need is his delight.

My father wants me to build a massive place for my new bride. I know that the beauty of the place is going to dazzle my sweetheart. I can hardly wait to see the look on her face. She grew up in desperate poverty. She is about to be ushered into lavish splendor. Just thinking about it brings me such joy.

## The Case of the Jealous Lover

*It is taking a long time to build the mansion because of the precious materials used in the construction. If a material exists anywhere in the world that is of high quality, I am having it brought in. My design is opulent but not gaudy.*

*The floors of the mansion are made of precious stone with gold inlaid accents. The walls are semi-precious jewels. The ceilings are works of art. To look up is to peer into heaven. Angels, embroidered into the ceiling tapestries, hover over each room. They symbolize the protection and safety that the house provides. I want my beloved to know that she is safe in this house.*

*The gates to the mansion are so costly that I know people have come just to see the artistry of them. I have built the mansion with perfect dimensions and angles. It is startlingly beautiful.*

*To accent the approach to the mansion, I have built a fence around the property. Each side has a three-gate access. Each set of three gates is made of a different kind of pearl. The north gates have a rose color, and the east gates have an aquamarine color. The west gates are a rare sand-colored pearl, and the south gates are made of black pearl. The south gates are my favorites. That black, almost iridescent, color with a metallic sheen makes those gates stand out.*

## "I Have a Surprise"

Where I live, we don't have a wedding day—we have wedding seasons. The ceremony is only part of the whole experience of getting married. The agenda of a wedding is designed to produce maximum enjoyment for both parties, their families, and their friends.

After a young man's intended bride accepts his proposal, he has to leave, just like I did, and prepare a home for his bride. She has to wait for his return. But her waiting time is filled with excitement. Because she doesn't know the day or hour of his return, she has to remain ready.

Now, she knows he will be coming in the evening. So, every evening she puts her wedding dress on. Her ears perk up at every sound. Her friends all know that his coming will be a surprise, so they check with her to make sure she remains ready.

When the father of a bridegroom is satisfied that his son has made the proper provisions for marriage, he gives his son permission to go and get his bride. This is the high point of the marriage season. The son has trumpeters on notice for that day. They go before the son to the bride's house and blow their trumpets. When the bride hears those trumpets, she must quickly set everything in order.

Her bridesmaids light their lanterns and line the street leading up to the bride's home, creating a lighted pathway. The bridesmaids have great *responsibility in this. They have to make sure that the wicks of their lamps are trimmed for maximum light production. They also have to make sure their lamps are burning brightly. They cannot afford to wait to light their lamps when the trumpets sound because it will take too long. They definitely don't want to miss their opportunity to shine during the procession.*

*It is an intense time for everyone involved. The bride cannot afford to let her husband catch her unprepared. She has to look perfect for him. This will be the first time since he left that he will see her. She has to be beautiful and dressed to perfection to win his heart all over again.*

*The bridesmaids have to be ready in order to get into the wedding dinner. Any maid who does not have a burning lantern is not permitted into the wedding dinner. To be turned away could be the most embarrassing moment in a young lady's life. No matter whose wedding it is, there are always some bridesmaids who don't take their responsibility seriously and don't get into the wedding feast.*

*This is how marriages are performed in our culture, but my marriage is going to be grander and more lavish than any marriage before it.*

*My bride doesn't know it, but I am a prince, heir to the throne, and I am going to take her to a place*

*beyond her wildest dreams. I have so concealed my
identity from her that she has no idea that I am not
a commoner like herself.*

*But wait! I just received a startling report from
my servants whom I have assigned to protect her
during my absence. My bride has run off with another man! I don't want to believe it. This could
not be happening to me now. I can't have been betrayed, not by her. I have to get to the bottom of
this.*

### PRACTICAL APPLICATION

In 1 Corinthians 13, often referred to as the
Love Chapter, the apostle Paul wrote the following:

> *For now we see in a mirror dimly, but then
> face to face; now I know in part, but then I
> shall know fully just as I also have been fully
> known.*                              *(verse 12)*

The King James translation of this verse is
helpful, too. It says, *"For now we see through a
glass, darkly; but then face to face: now I know in
part; but then shall I know even as also I am
known."* This is an awesome statement, especially
coming from Paul, who had dedicated his entire

life after his conversion to the pursuit of God, and who already had been shown spiritual revelations and visions.

Paul had seen things that were too wonderful to utter (2 Corinthians 12:1–4). I believe that Paul was head and shoulders above the other apostles in understanding. Peter, in one of his epistles, spoke of Paul's wisdom (2 Peter 3:15–16). Paul's desire was to be just like the Lord. Yet he had to admit that all of his knowledge and learning and encounters with God still left him with mere tidbits of understanding and knowledge about the Lord. All he could see were mere shadows of God's splendor.

The jealous lover's bride did not know everything about him. She had no idea that he was a prince. He had hidden his true identity from her, but he knew that one day she would be overwhelmed by all he would give her. He wanted to surprise her.

In the Christian life, God desires that we patiently wait for His surprise return. He wants us to be ready, with our lanterns lit for His arrival. (See Matthew 25:1–13.) He also wants us to look forward to the abundant blessings that He has in store for us. While we wait here on earth, He is preparing a place in heaven for each of His children. *"I go to prepare a place for you,"* said Christ in John 14:2.

## "I Have a Surprise"

When that place is completed, Christ will return for His church, and the two will be united for eternity.

But just as He did with Paul, God does not tell us everything about Himself. For the time being, we only *"know in part"* (1 Corinthians 13:12). We will not take part in the Marriage Supper of the Lamb (Revelation 19:9) until our place in heaven has been prepared and Christ returns to take His church as His bride.

Unfortunately, when people are left in the dark, they tend to think the worst and not the best. They start imagining all kinds of things that would never actually happen. Here is where faith comes in. If we have faith, we will be assured that God will do what is best for us.

Even though we can only *"know in part"* now, God desires to reveal Himself to us as we seek Him with all our hearts. He wants to give us a glimpse of His majesty, and to have our lives reflect His glory.

Moses had an experience with the Lord that was similar to Paul's. To begin with, God had called Moses to service by using a burning bush at the base of Mount Horeb. (See Exodus 3:1–10.) The bush caught Moses' attention because it was in flames but didn't burn up. Moses was called for the great work of leading God's people. The Lord performed some miracles to encourage Moses to believe Him in every situation.

Thirty chapters later, Moses was back at the same mountain at which God had called him. The Lord was giving him some instructions concerning the people, and he was interceding on their behalf. Moses was now a seasoned servant of God. He skillfully and faithfully prayed for the people. Because of his relationship with the Father, the disobedience of the people notwithstanding, Moses was granted every request he made.

Moses took full advantage of his access to God, and in so doing, he taught us a wonderful lesson. Whenever you have the attention of God, you should never end the conversation. Stay until He is finished. Ask until He closes the door. Receive from the Lord until He shuts off the fountain. Never leave blessings on the table. Your attitude should be, "All that God has for me, I want."

Toward the end of their time together, Moses asked God for one more thing: "I beg You, Lord, show me Your glory!" (See Exodus 33:18.) That got God's attention. Moses' request was of a different sort than anything else that he'd asked of God before. All his other requests were made in the course of doing business for the kingdom of God. But this one was strictly for his relationship with God.

Perhaps you can imagine a present-day Moses saying to God, "This time, Lord, I am not asking for food on the table, clothes for my children, rent money, or a job. I am asking You to reveal Yourself to me. I want to know You for who You are. I want to be close to You. I am not asking this time for You to work on my behalf. My request is not directed toward Your miracle-working power. I want to be intimate with You."

I am convinced that too many believers spend their entire time with the Lord in a business partnership instead of a personal relationship. They treat the Lord in much the same way that husbands and wives do who, amid the bills, dental appointments, mortgage payments, and careers, have forgotten the real reason that they married.

The Lord is not an abstract concept. He is not a philosophical idea. He is a person with feelings. He wants to be loved and considered. He is interested in us and wants us to be interested in Him.

Any believer who only sees the Lord as a ticket out of this troubled world or as an exemption from hell misses the best of who He is.

If you only know enough about the Lord to say that you're saved, as precious as that fact is, you've misunderstood His real purpose. God's intention is not just to rescue you; He also wants to be in a covenant relationship with you.

This is why the institution of marriage is so important to the Lord. The image of the Bridegroom represents the very essence of what the Lord is and wants to be to us. The Lord will return for His church, and after that we will be married to Him as His bride.

After Moses asked to see God's glory, God told him to go up the mountain in the morning. The Lord gave Moses several instructions before granting Moses' request. However, once Moses was on top of the mountain, God did grant his request, because He was pleased to reveal His glory to someone who was so interested in Him.

Pay close attention to the passage we're considering here. Moses did not make a request to see another miracle. He had seen some awesome miracles before. He was asking God to unveil His glory and reveal His essential nature. Moses had an idea that there was much more to the Lord than what he had experienced already.

Wouldn't it be wonderful if believers today understood that there is more to God than "meets the eye"? There is more to the Lord than just going to church, singing in the choir, going to work under His protection, and eating food blessed by Him. These things are not all that the Lord has to offer. He wants to reveal Himself to us as we earnestly seek to know Him; He wants His glory to be reflected in our lives. Furthermore, just as the jealous lover was building a splendid place for his new bride, Christ is building a mansion for each of us in heaven (John 14:2 NKJV), and the New Jerusalem will be perfectly designed for God's people. (See Revelation 21:10–22:5.) God wants you to experience these blessings.

Deuteronomy 29:29 states that there are some secret things that belong to the Lord: *"The secret things belong to the LORD our God, but the things revealed belong to us and to our sons forever."* A lifetime of study, prayer, and devotion will not reveal to you all that God is. But the last part of this verse encourages the believer by suggesting that there are some things the Lord has revealed and will reveal to those who are willing to go beyond the doorway of their salvation.

As I said earlier, the Lord granted Moses' request to see His glory, though He reminded Moses that no human had ever seen His face and lived (Exodus 33:20). It is not my purpose here to review the entire story, but there are some interesting features that should be explored. First, after the request was made, the Lord declared that there was *"a place"* beside Him (verse 21). Think about it. All that time, Moses was leading an entire nation of people called the children of God. But here the Lord said to him, "I have a special place beside Me."

God, help us to desire that place next to You.

Second, the Lord revealed that if He granted the request Moses had made without preparing him, he would be blown off the mountain. So, the Lord wedged Moses in the cleft of the rock.

But even that was not sufficient. The Lord told Moses that in order to comply with his request and in order that Moses might live to tell about it, the Lord would have to cover him with His hand.

Just that touch from God would have been worth the trip up the mountain! But God told Moses, "I'll cover you with My hand." Cover me, Lord!

Third, after all this preparation, the Lord then told Moses His plan. The Lord would let His glory pass before Moses while His hand covered him and protected him from that much holiness and power. Then the Lord would take His hand off Moses and allow him to see His *"back parts"* (Exodus 33:23 KJV).

The translators of the King James Version had difficulty finding a suitable English word or group of words to describe what God was referring to here. Scholars have told me that there is no easy way to translate this. The best way to describe the *"back parts"* of God is to say that what Moses actually saw was what was left behind after the glory had been there and gone.

## "I Have a Surprise"

Yet what he did see was so powerful that his face shone like an illuminated light bulb. The glory of the Lord was radiant upon his face—so much so that the Israelites were afraid to come near him. This radiance occurred every time Moses went into the presence of the Lord, and gradually faded away when Moses left the presence of the Lord. Therefore, from that day on, Moses put a veil over his face after meeting with God and reporting God's instructions to the people, because he did not want the children of Israel to witness the glory of the Lord fading from his face. (See Exodus 34:29–35; 2 Corinthians 3:7–8, 13.)

What would the kingdom of God be like today if every believer was determined not to be seen without the glory of the Lord upon his life? What a testimony to the power and majesty of God we would give!

Even so, we must realize that God is saving the fullness of His revelation of Himself for the future—when we go to be with Him forever. In the examples we have just looked at, Paul and Moses saw things from the Lord that the average believer never sees. Yet even Paul saw these things only *"dimly"* (1 Corinthians 13:12), and Moses saw only "leftover" glory. They saw all that they were allowed to see.

## The Case of the Jealous Lover

Now, if *"eye has not seen, nor ear heard, nor have entered into the heart of man the things which God has prepared for those who love Him"* (1 Corinthians 2:9 NKJV), what kind of surprise is the Lord preparing for us? The Bible gives us some clues, but for now, like Paul, we only *"see in a mirror dimly"* and *"know in part"* (1 Corinthians 13:12) what God has in store for us. He will indeed reveal Himself to us in full, but only if we have faith in Him until that time.

The key to receiving this revelation of God is faith. There is no way to please the Lord without living by faith (Hebrews 11:6). By faith we believe in Him, though we do not know everything about Him. He will not tell us everything because, on the one hand, it would be too much for us if He did, and on the other hand, He wants to surprise us. Having faith in God means having confidence in His power to deliver you and having an assurance that He will do what is best for you.

Recall that the jealous lover's proposal had been accepted; his beloved had taken the wine that he had offered. But she was apprehensive about his return. Would he really come back for her? Her apprehension was great, and it was difficult to wait.

Similarly, God is our Jealous Lover who is frustrated by our tendency to stray from Him, though we have accepted Him as Savior. Will you wait for Him? Will you have faith that He will fulfill for you all that He has promised?

Let me bring this chapter to a close with one of my favorite Scriptures: *"For if while we were enemies, we were reconciled to God through the death of His Son, much more, having been reconciled, we shall be saved by His life"* (Romans 5:10). My translation of this verse is as follows: if Christ was willing to perform that awesome and supreme work at Calvary for us at a time when we hated Him, what will He do for us now that we are family?

> *But as it is, [we] desire a better country, that is a heavenly one. Therefore God is not ashamed to be called [our] God; for He has prepared a city for [us].* (Hebrews 11:16)

## A PRAYER

*Dear Lord, teach us to appreciate You not just for the things that You do for us, but also for who You are. Help us to get rid of all selfishness, even the kind that's wrapped up in prayer requests. Help us to understand the value of relationship, commitment, and patience. And Lord, while You're helping us to relate to You better, help us to draw closer to our families, as well. In Jesus' name, I pray.*

*Chapter Nine*

## *"I Am Furious!"*

*Chapter Nine*

# "*I Am Furious!*"

*I* can't believe my ears. My servants have to be mistaken. Not my beloved—not the woman I brought out of nowhere into my world. She couldn't be unfaithful, could she?

*Why? How? How could she do this? How could she do this to me, after all I have done for her? I have given her my best, my all. I have talked to her for hours and have told her constantly how much I love her. I have held her close to me and have whispered to her my love for her. She is still the flower of my field and the star of my sky. I love her, and yet she walks on my feelings with no more concern than she would have after stepping on an ant. I am furious!*

## The Case of the Jealous Lover

*My bride has run off with another man. In broad daylight she has just run off with some man she met on the street. I sent her flowers and messages; I came to see her every day before I proposed to her. I took her out and showed her a good time. And she can leave me for some man who just beckoned to her—that's all? My servants told me that he took her captive at his will. He just snapped his fingers, and she came running.*

*My father has told me about this man: he is a scoundrel. His reputation is horrible. He is an abuser and liar; he steals, kills, and destroys everything he puts his hands on. He is a con artist and shyster—a smooth-talking hustler. His claim to fame is his looks. He goes through women just like a snake that slithers through grass.*

*Oh, I hate him. I hate everything about him. He has a foul mouth and a vile personality. He cares only about himself and thinks that the universe should worship him.*

*When I first heard about what my beloved has done, I got so angry that I roared like a lion and stomped my feet until the earth shook beneath me. My wrath was hot, and I saw the need to punish her. But in my great patience, I remembered who she is and where she came from.*

*I tried to consider that she is emotionally fragile, vulnerable, and easily persuaded. Like blades of grass and wildflowers in a field, she can be blown aside by the wind or left crushed by the lightest footstep. But these thoughts have not completely subdued my anger. I cannot understand how she can take my love and trample on it as if it were garbage.*

*I have tried to figure out what is going on. Doesn't she know I love her and adore her? I had overlooked others to be with her exclusively. Doesn't she remember where I found her? She is not popular. There is not a long line of men standing at her door hoping to get to see her. She is hated and taunted by her neighbors.*

*She had not been attractive until she met me. I fixed her up and took her to the best places. Before I found her, people had teased her about how plain and unattractive she looked. Her own brothers had been ashamed of her until I started helping her with her appearance.*

*Then everyone noticed how good she looked. They would say to her, "That man has done something for you! You look so beautiful. Keep praising him, honey. Whatever you do, don't let that man get away."*

*I have never been unfaithful to her. I had stopped looking when I found her. My pain is deep. I am wounded. Not just because she has left me, but also because she has left me for so little.*

*What does that make me? Am I no better to her than a street hustler? Can't I get any more respect than that? What kind of woman would turn down someone like me for that scoundrel she has run off with?*

*To top it all off, my beloved is committing the crime of adultery. Although we are only engaged to be married, in our society this has the same legal status as marriage, and adultery is a crime punishable by stoning. An offense of this nature against the royal family cannot be overlooked. But can I watch my beloved die as stones are hurled at her without mercy?*

*I know I have to do something about this. I cannot let this go on! It is time for action.*

## PRACTICAL APPLICATION

People can really ruin a good thing, can't they? How often have you observed people who were just about to come into a time of great prosperity and happiness, but who destroyed the chance with their own hands? You looked at them and wondered how they could do such a thing.

Human beings have a unique way of contradicting logic, and their actions so often defy explanation. For example, it seems as if people in many marriages are mismatched. Outgoing, life-loving people seem to be attracted to introverted recluses. People who have great passion and affection end up marrying stoic and emotionally dead people. You would think that people would know better than to marry individuals who are incompatible with them, but apparently they don't.

Then there are the people who are attracted to rogue, vile, and contemptible individuals. I am sure there is a clinical category for this kind of person. Such a person is too timid to live a wild, undisciplined life but is turned on by those who do. This type of person lives in a fantasy world but soon discovers, after marriage, that a bad person is a bad person. He or she learns, too late to avoid being damaged, that such flawed behavior lacks all resemblance to good judgment.

The saddest category of illogical personalities is the self-destructive one. A person with this type of personality is burdened with a prevailing mind-set that hinders him from accepting good things in his life. He actually believes that his lot in life is to be miserable. He is comfortable being miserable. He makes others around him miserable because he is devoted to being unhappy. This type of person actively sabotages all good things in his life. He pushes people away from him who would be good for him. He complains about the abuse he suffers, but he refuses to do anything about it.

Wives in this category constantly talk about how badly their husbands are treating them. It is evident that they are being physically abused, but they remain in their bad relationships and get beaten again. When others try to intervene on their behalf, these women turn on their would-be helpers. When asked why, they boldly and irrationally say, "Leave him alone. You just don't understand. He is really a good person. He hits me because he loves me." Perplexed, the rescuers leave, shaking their heads, wondering how the wives could think in this way.

Men of this type are just as self-destructive. They have the ability to find good, virtuous women who are interested in them. But, somehow, before they can get to the altar, they destroy the relationship. They are deeply remorseful afterward but are at a loss to explain their bad behavior. Their problem, like that of all in this category, is that they hate themselves. They have accepted the notion that they are no good and are unworthy of happiness.

These people are frustrating to be around. You can see their potential; they are talented and could do wonderful things for society. You know they could be happy, but no matter how you try to help them, they mess it up somehow.

## "I Am Furious!"

You can give them a job. They will do well for a while, but by their behavior they will make you fire them before long. You can befriend them. They will stay with the relationship until you make any demands on them. Then, in the middle of the night, they'll slip away, never to be seen again. They will destroy themselves and everything around them if given a chance.

A casual observer encountering this behavior would simply write these people off as unsalvageable. On the surface, they do seem to be too difficult to deal with. But they cannot be written off. These are living, breathing creations of God. They have souls and should not be thrown away. They need help.

Of all the people who are afflicted with flawed behavior, these people can really make you furious—not angry, but furious! They do so by making you fall in love with them. They have good qualities and in many cases are likable for a while. Then they do something crazy and leave you high and dry. You become furious because they have touched your heart. A person who is bad to the core would not have had the same effect on you.

They wonder why you are so enraged. They think that you should not be affected because, as they put it, they are only hurting themselves.

## The Case of the Jealous Lover

You know better, though. They are hurting
everyone around them. It is aggravating to watch
them waste their potential, because while they are
wasting theirs, they are wasting yours, too, by
taking up your time and energy.

### Israel's "Slave Mentality"

The Israelites were acting in this way when
they turned away from God after He had brought
them out of Egypt. Let's look at the story in Exodus 32:

> Then the LORD spoke to Moses, "Go down at
> once, for your people, whom you brought up
> from the land of Egypt, have corrupted them-
> selves. They have quickly turned aside from
> the way which I commanded them. They have
> made for themselves a molten calf, and have
> worshiped it, and have sacrificed to it, and
> said, 'This is your god, O Israel, who brought
> you up from the land of Egypt!'" And the
> LORD said to Moses, "I have seen this people,
> and behold, they are an obstinate people. Now
> then let Me alone, that My anger may burn
> against them, and that I may destroy them;
> and I will make of you a great nation." Then
> Moses entreated the LORD his God, and said,
> "O LORD, why doth Thine anger burn against

## "I Am Furious!"

*Thy people whom Thou hast brought out from the land of Egypt with great power and with a mighty hand? Why should the Egyptians speak, saying, 'With evil intent He brought them out to kill them in the mountains and to destroy them from the face of the earth'? Turn from Thy burning anger and change Thy mind about doing harm to Thy people. Remember Abraham, Isaac, and Israel, Thy servants to whom Thou didst swear by Thyself, and didst say to them, 'I will multiply your descendants as the stars of the heavens, and all this land of which I have spoken I will give to your descendants, and they shall inherit it forever.'" So the LORD changed His mind about the harm which He said He would do to His people. (Exodus 32:7–14)*

God was angry—angry because the people for whom He had done so much were destroying His work so quickly. In response, God told Moses to step aside while He destroyed the people of Israel. His intention was to wipe them out and repopulate His kingdom with Moses' offspring. Fortunately for them, Moses was dedicated to his job as an intercessor.

The people of Israel, held captive and enslaved by the Egyptians, had been set free from that bondage by the mighty hand of God. They were to enter into the Promised Land. Their deliverance had been orchestrated by God and had been designed to build character in them. Because of their rebellion, however, He had to take them on the long route to the Promised Land. This would give them an opportunity to change their mind-set from one of slavery to one of freedom as God's people.

God knew that slavery had altered their thinking and their value system. The conditions had been poor in Egypt. The people had had to make downward adjustments in their expectations in order to survive. They had been in a kindness drought. Little sprinkles of kindness offered to them had been significant, for one day had been exactly like the day before it. They had had nothing to look forward to but more slavery.

When the mighty hand of God liberated them, their bodies were removed from Egypt, but their minds were not changed that easily. They walked around free but didn't enjoy their freedom. They had been conditioned to believe that their lot in life was to be slaves.

### A Faith Odyssey

The Lord had to take them on a faith odyssey. For decades they walked through a barren wilderness. No, God wasn't being cruel; they needed to have their faith rebuilt. He had to prove to them that He was all the help they required. Clearly, if God could keep them under His protection in a desperate situation, they could be kept under His protection in any situation.

During their wanderings, miracles both obvious and obscure happened to them. The obvious miracles were the water out of the rock (Exodus 17:6; Numbers 20:11), manna from heaven (Exodus 16:4–5), and quail from the sea (Numbers 11:31). The obscure ones were the daily adjustments made to their clothing and shoes. Children grow, and adults' bodies alter over time, yet their clothes never wore out and did not become too tight or loose for them. Their God took care of every detail of life.

The Israelites faced enemy nations, too. These warring nations came against Israel with sophisticated weapons and years of experience in warfare. Israel only had years of experience as slaves. The only fighting they had done had been between themselves. But they did have God. As it turned out, warlike, brutish nations, fine-tuned for battle, were no match for a slavery-accustomed, unorganized, inexperienced nation that had God on its side.

God made the difference. He proved His power over and over again. But the wilderness was, after all, a training ground for Israel. God never intended for His children to go from slavery in Egypt to end-less wanderings in a barren wilderness. His plan for them was that they would occupy *"a land flowing with milk and honey"* (Exodus 3:8). He wanted them to *"prosper and be in good health"* (3 John 1:2). He planned that His people would be the first and not the last (Deuteronomy 28:13), and that their children would be blessed.

He would work it out so that His children would possess houses they had not built and vine-yards they had not planted, and would harvest crops from fields they had not plowed. (See Joshua 24:13.) While marching through the wilderness, they couldn't imagine the place at the end of their journey. The wilderness certainly looked like just a wilderness to them. One rock looked like the other; the monotony was overwhelming.

But that's the beauty of walking by faith. The Lord doesn't provide all the details of His plan to us. He wants us to trust Him instead.

Let's explore now the reasons why the people of Israel ended up in their wilderness experience and why God was so angry with them.

### Fears and Misgivings

God had walked Israel to the very edge of blessings. The people had been just a river's width away from their own land. The Lord spoke to Moses and told him to go in and possess the land.

In Numbers 13, we read that God commanded Moses to send spies into the land. Moses chose the spies from among the leaders of every tribe. These men were influential in their respective districts. Their endorsement would weigh heavily on the thinking of their constituents. If they approved of going in and taking the land, Israel would go in and possess the land. If they disapproved, then Israel would not go in and possess the land.

The spies went to the land in order to *"see what the land is like; [and to] see...what the people are like who live there, whether they are strong or weak, many or few"* (Numbers 13:18). Upon their return, the spies were able to verify that the land was as God had said. They went there, however, with the mind-set of slaves. Instead of looking at the potential, they worried about the risks. If the spies had been wise, they would have done what the dove did during Noah's time.

The dove was released three times from the ark by Noah to see if the land had emerged from the floodwaters. The third time, when the dove found that the land was available, it never returned to the ark to let Noah know what it had found. The dove was too busy enjoying its freedom. (See Genesis 8:6–12.)

The twelve men of Israel observed the Promised Land and brought back examples of its bounty. However, most of them had seen the land through the eyes of fear. Had they looked at the same situation with eyes of faith, they would have returned with a victory report.

When the twelve spies returned to the camp of Israel, about six hundred thousand men, not counting women and children, were waiting for their report. God had brought them to this spot because He wanted them to move from a "wilderness" experience to a "possess the land" experience. He had celebration, victory, and fresh beginnings planned for them. He was ready; Moses and the people were ready to move. They all were waiting for the report of the spies.

The twelve men of renown, leaders in their districts and mighty men, began their report. They acknowledged that the land did have all the wonderful things God had said it had. They brought back examples of the fine fruit and other bounties the land provided. Joshua and Caleb, two of the spies, declared that Israel could take the land. But the other ten spies had brought back fears and misgivings along with the fruit and bounties.

## "I Am Furious!"

### A Negative Mind-Set

The report of these ten spies shows how negative their mind-set was. Remember, God had told them to go and possess the land. He had never required that they qualify His word. They simply had to obey. The fact that God had said, "Go and possess the land," ruled out failure for this venture. If failure were an option, the Lord would have phrased His command differently. If the statement from God was, "Go and try to possess the land," then the people would have had reason for being uncertain.

I am convinced that these ten spies were afraid of change and development. It could be that they really didn't want to move to the next level with God. Life was already much different from what they had been used to in Egypt. Probably, their emotions were troubled because of the radical events associated with their freedom.

Israel missed the point because they could not get rid of the notion that they could live no better than slaves could live. What God intended to be a glorious day of improvement turned into a day of disobedience and forfeited blessings.

The reality of this story is that the people were too timid and had too poor of an opinion of themselves to enjoy the plans God had for them. It seems clear to me that they could not imagine living as well and prospering as much as God had envisioned that they live and prosper.

By the time the ten spies had finished telling the Israelites about the dangers associated with the new land, all the excitement of the people had disappeared. The whole mood of the event turned from triumph to tragedy. What is amazing about this story is how easily a very small segment of the population was able to undo all the teaching and leadership of God's man of action, Moses.

### A Heart Problem

An examination of the report exposes the character of the spies' heart problem. The spies admitted that the land was as wealthy as God had said. They said, *"We went in to the land where you sent us; and it certainly does flow with milk and honey, and this is its fruit"* (Numbers 13:27). It was the next word, *"nevertheless"* (verse 28), that killed the event. When they said *"nevertheless,"* they were saying, "Forget what we just told you. Forget the dream, and get real. We will never have this land no matter how lush and rich it is."

The first aspect of their problem was their inclination to see the negative in a positive situation.

They verified that the land was wealthy but concluded that it was not for them.

The second aspect of their problem was that they were easily intimidated and were too much in awe of their enemies. They said in Numbers 13:28, *"The people who live in the land are strong, and the cities are fortified and very large; and moreover, we saw the descendants of Anak there."* The descendents of Anak were giants. Their average height was in the seven-foot range.

The spies' report was filled with information about their enemies, but it contained no mention of the attributes of their God. They knew so much about their enemies. Why didn't they know as much about their God who had done great miracles for them? Why didn't they boast about His power? It is a shame that we can be spokespersons for our enemies but mute about our God.

Let me put this story into perspective for us today. Here Israel talked so much about their enemies and so little about their God. God wants us to have complete love and confidence in Him instead of dwelling on how overwhelming our problems and circumstances—our enemies, in a sense—are.

In a related way, one of the best ways to put a strain on a love relationship is to talk more about another man or woman than you talk about your companion. No spouse wants to hear about some other man or woman. Your companion wants to know that he or she has all your attention, devotion, and love. To please your companion, you need to boast about him or her. In other words, your companion needs to know that he or she is your champion.

The third and final aspect of the spies' heart problem was their lack of esteem. I am not a proponent of telling people they have to build their self-esteem. That is why I didn't call their problem a self-esteem problem. I like to substitute another word for *self-esteem*. I think what they needed then and what we need now is *God-esteem!* The question, therefore, is not "How well do you think of yourself?" but "How well do you think of your God?"

Israel had low God-esteem. The last part of their report is both gruesome and pitiful, and is lacking in God-esteem. Numbers 13:32–33 says,

*So they gave out to the sons of Israel a bad report of the land which they had spied out, saying, "The land through which we have gone, in spying it out, is a land that devours its inhabitants; and all the people whom we saw in it are men of great size. There also we saw the Nephilim (the sons of Anak are part of the Nephilim); and we became like grasshoppers in our own sight, and so we were in their sight."*

They were afraid of the land: *"The land...is a land that devours its inhabitants."* They were afraid of the people there: *"And all the people whom we saw in it are men of great size."* And finally, they were ashamed of themselves: *"And we became like grasshoppers in our own sight, and so we were in their sight."* Notice that the spies, who never interviewed the enemy, were willing to assign thoughts to their enemy. They presumed to imagine what the enemy must have been thinking. They concluded that their enemy thought of Israel as grasshoppers, as bugs to be crushed.

But in fact, just the opposite was probably true. See what Rahab said to another set of Israel's spies in Joshua 2:9–11 when the Israelites came to conquer Jericho:

*I know that the LORD has given you the land, and that the terror of you has fallen on us, and that all the inhabitants of the land have melted away before you. For we have heard how the LORD dried up the water of the Red Sea before you when you came out of Egypt, and what you did to the two kings of the Amorites who were beyond the Jordan, to Sihon and Og, whom you utterly destroyed. And*

*when we heard it, our hearts melted and no
courage remained in any man any longer because of you; for the LORD your God, He is God
in heaven above and on earth beneath.*

Here was Israel, walking around crying,
moaning, and feeling sorry for themselves. At the
same time, their enemies were shaking in their
boots because of the power of the testimony of
what God had done for Israel. God defeated Israel's enemies using the testimony of His goodness
to Israel. The cruel joke is that everyone except
Israel knew that Israel was blessed.

### When God Hurts

Remember that the jealous lover was very
hurt by his beloved's unfaithfulness; he was furious! Likewise, it's not hard to understand why
God was so angry. In a way, He was hurt because
His loved ones were so eager to talk about and
trust in the power of their enemies. Even today,
God sees us overawed by the Devil's power and
tricks again and again, though Jesus warned us
that Satan is a liar and a con artist (see John 8:44)
and the Bible tells us, *"Greater is He who is in you
than he who is in the world"* (1 John 4:4). The Lord
expects the same kind of respect and devotion from

each of us as a husband or wife expects from his or her companion. God has feelings, too.

After hearing the whimpering of ten men, the people of Israel suddenly went from being thrilled and festive to somber and sullen. Over six hundred thousand men became distraught and failed to believe the report of the Lord over the majority opinion of such an insignificant twelve-member human committee.

There is still more evidence of Israel's self-destructive heart problem in this passage. The Israelites reacted in an inordinate way to what they heard. When the spies finished their report, the people reacted with great alarm and despair. They had been upbeat and positive until the report came out. Then Israel went into deep depression. Numbers 14 reveals that Israel, upon hearing the news, cried all night long (verse 1). God had expected to hear singing and shouting and praise in the camp that night. Instead, He heard crying and moaning as though someone great had died among them.

It gets worse as we go further into the chapter. As the depression progressed, Israel went from crying all night to murmuring and complaining against the leadership. Then they had a death wish, and finally they accused God of having had evil intentions toward them all along.

## The Case of the Jealous Lover

### Fear rather than Faith

The effect of ten men's fearful report was devastating to Israel and nullified God's word in their hearts. God had said, "You can have it," and a mere ten men said, "No, we cannot." As a result, over half a million men believed ten men who were operating in fear rather than in faith. They chose men over the mighty God! This was pitiful.

Ten men in one day successfully suspended for thirty-eight more years what God had planned to do for Israel that day. They could have been living in their blessing almost forty years before they did—all because they couldn't believe that something this good could happen to them. Isn't this just like so many people today?

The children of Israel surrendered their future, their wealth, and their place in the world because of their destructive mind-set. They were on the path of blessing and ended up on the treadmill of a wilderness existence. The negative report of ten men destroyed a whole nation's confidence and trust in God.

How could ten men have this much influence over so great a congregation? The answer is found in who the spies were. They represented those who walk by sight and not by faith. (Compare 2

Corinthians 5:7.) The spies did for Israel what our senses do for us. What we can see, hear, smell, taste, and feel tells us what is real and possible for us. But God is not restricted by what our senses tell us. He can do for us what we would never have imagined. If Israel had recognized this fact, they would have entered the Promised Land that very day.

This story is so tragic. The Israelites' disobedience had the same effect as shooting oneself in the foot. This kind of destructive behavior not only inflicts injury on oneself, but it also affects the lives of others. (See Numbers 14:33.)

### Of "Trust Abuse" and Trust in God

I've heard a number of preachers speak on this passage concerning Israel's failure to obey God. They focus on the rebellious nature of the children of Israel. There was rebellion, but why were they like this?

When I was pondering this problem, I thought about my earlier examples of self-destructive personality disorders and how people in general relate to God. Although I understand that people are like this, it still doesn't make sense to me that anyone would spurn the love of God. Why would anyone refuse to accept His care?

I suggest that the people of Israel were like this because of deficiencies in their character. Very simply, they didn't trust God. It is precisely at this point that the root of the problem may be found.

Many people today have a hard time trusting anybody because they've been so abused in the past; their lack of trust is a reactionary response to having been betrayed. It is impossible to live without having to trust somebody even when you don't want to, for there are too many details of life that cannot be handled alone. But when you have to trust someone who isn't trustworthy, you suffer loss. People everywhere are suffering from the pain of "trust abuse." They tried to believe in somebody and got hurt for it.

In general, children trust their parents, workers trust their employers, patients trust their doctors, and airline passengers trust their pilots. Tragically, some children are molested, workers are fired without reason or warning, patients do not get well, and things go wrong on airplanes. People affected by these crises, still hurting from a badly shaken confidence in people, are asked to trust in God. The concept seems plausible to them, but they will not trust because they are wounded. They have become cynical and unbelieving to the point that they will not respond to the plain evidence of God's faithfulness. They are emotionally crippled. They need a healing that only God can provide.

The Bible says in Ephesians 3:20, "[God] *is able to do exceeding abundantly beyond all that we ask or think, according to the power that works within us.*" God has the power *"to do"*; we need the power to believe Him.

In order to have a workable relationship with God, you must stop depending on your own thoughts and abilities and trust in God's power instead. This point will never be made clearer than it is made by the story of the Israelites' wilderness experience. Faith in God, trusting Him, is the key to a successful relationship with Him. Proverbs 3:5–6 says, *"Trust in the LORD with all your heart, and do not lean on your own understanding. In all your ways acknowledge Him, and He will make your paths straight."*

Of all the things about God that we can be thankful for, His patience and understanding should rank at the top of the list. The Lord was furious with Israel because of their lack of faith. They might have known Him better and trusted Him more. But they didn't. However, the Lord understood that they were like flowers that appear for a moment and fade away. (See James 1:11.) God still had plans for His people, to bring them into the Promised Land. The next generation would enter in, because of the mercy and love of God.

Similarly, the jealous lover was furious with his beloved for running off with another man. She had failed to trust him entirely. But the jealous lover understood where she had come from. She had been abandoned over and over again, so it was difficult for her to trust at all.

Perhaps this is much like your own life story or that of someone you know. You may have difficulty trusting others because your trust has been abused again and again. In this case, the important things to recognize are that *"God is love"* (1 John 4:8, 16) and *"love never fails"* (1 Corinthians 13:8). God loves you and will be faithful to you (1 Corinthians 1:9); He will not hurt you. Trust in Him (Psalm 37:5).

In His patience, God put His plans on hold and had the people of Israel walk in the wilderness long enough for them to get rid of their fear and their lack of trust. The next generation of Israel was then taken into the Promised Land. God does the same for people today. Where would we be without the mercy and understanding of God? We all, from time to time, have wounded the Lord with our lack of faith. Yet He remains faithful to us. He is, after all, a good God.

# "I Am Furious!"

## A PRAYER

*Dear Lord, I thank You for being so kind, understanding, and long-suffering with us. Often we fail to accept Your best because of our weaknesses. I pray, Lord, that You will help us all to trust You more and to depend on Your power rather than our own. Help us to overcome our feelings of inadequacy. Heal us of our disabilities, past hurts, and the abuses of the world.*

*Help us to see in ourselves what You see in us, so that we can love You more and serve You better. Set us free, Lord, from the curses of the past and from being held captive by fear of our enemies.*

*I worship You, Lord, because I know that You have begun a good work in us and that You will perform it and complete it to Your glory (Philippians 1:6). In Jesus' name, I pray.*

*Chapter Ten*

# *A Man of Sorrows*

*Chapter Ten*

# A Man of Sorrows

*He was despised and forsaken of men, a man of*
*sorrows, and acquainted with grief; and like one*
*from whom men hide their face, He was*
*despised, and we did not esteem Him.*
*—Isaiah 53:3*

*T*here is no trouble like love trouble. You
might imagine how low I feel. It is as if my
beloved has stripped me naked out in the
open before everybody. I am ashamed and embarrassed, and I feel like a fool.

I have heard my enemy, the trickster, laughing
out loud at my misfortune. He just enjoys watching
this happen to me. He has come to me with his fake
concern and has laughed at me.

## The Case of the Jealous Lover

"You knew what kind of woman she was from the beginning of the relationship," he told me. "You got her out of the gutter." He cut into me as a butcher slices meat.

The strange thing about it was that he was right, in a sense. I did remember where I'd found her. I thought that if I showed her real love, she would appreciate it. I just knew she would love me for being real with her. Nobody else had ever treated her as well as I had.

I have seen the way other men handled her; they treated her as if she were a tramp. They didn't mind slapping her around and forcing her to do their dirty work. And when they got tired of her and she no longer amused them, they left her on the side of the road.

Not me, though; I didn't want her to feel that I was using her. I gave her dignity and a sense of purpose. That was more than her own brothers were willing to do.

It would be easy for me to marry royalty. There are plenty of women who would go out of their way to please me. But I don't want them; I want her. I did not choose her because she is powerful or great. I chose her because she is small. I love her so much, and that's the truth.

It seems that the old saying is true: "Can the Ethiopian change his skin, or the leopard his spots?" Of course, the answer is no. My lover is no exception. It's just that I was convinced that my love was love enough to change her. I want the best for her, and that's why I am in so much pain since she has abandoned me.

It is not easy being rejected. I am a sorrowful man and am full of grief. My tears are my food both night and day. My plans for our lives together have become the blueprints of my torment. When she left me, it was as if something died in me. But I still believe that I can make the relationship work somehow.

I found out where she was and sent my servants there to get her. My servants brought her back to her home, but all the while, she kept telling them that she would go away again. When I heard about this, I didn't pay any attention to her talk; I was determined to change her. I made sure she knew that if she would just quit doing those wicked things and change the way she thought, I would have mercy on her and would multiply my forgiveness to her.

Well, I have had to multiply my forgiveness to keep up with the number of times she has left me. She goes along well for months at a time, but then the call of the wild grabs hold of her and she's gone. The other man has a spell on her. He can just take her captive at his will. As I said before, he just snaps his fingers, and off she goes.

# The Case of the Jealous Lover

*Strangely enough, her other lover hates her. He doesn't care about her or even want her. He just wants to get revenge on me. One time my servants went to get her back, and they found her standing on the auction block. Her strange lover had put her up for sale. She meant nothing more to him than a quick way to make money.*

*I was humiliated, but still I loved her. My servants stood in that crowd bidding against other men for my bride, offering money to redeem her. She never really appreciated my efforts. She would mumble under her breath, "I don't know why you keep bothering with me. I am the way I am, and I will not change."*

*How can she say things like that to me? It is as if something has control of her mind. I believe that even when she does the right thing, evil is always present with her. She is pitiful, and I mourn her betrayal. Her heart is deceitful and extremely wicked, but she doesn't know it.*

*She has not changed, no matter what I have done. My servants played music for her, but she would not dance. They cried, but she would not mourn. Her demeanor is like a cold winter storm.*

*She is in trouble. She will soon be stoned to death. The trickster hates me so much that, in order to get to me, he has reported my bride to the authorities so that she will be executed by stoning.*

## A Man of Sorrows

*They will be happy to carry out the punishment in order to get at me, because they have the same nature as the trickster. I can't help feeling as if I have to shock my bride into realizing that the love she had with me was real. I have to do something.*

* * *

*I went to my father, asking him what I should do. We talked about the situation for three hours. I cried and talked and moaned over her. My father was deeply moved. I was so intense that bloody sweat began to cover my body. I struggled with the decision to rescue her at all costs. My father told me that his will for me was that I take the necessary steps to bring this situation to a conclusion once and for all. He told me that, in order to win her heart back to myself once and for all, I will have to take her place in death. It was not easy for him to ask me to lay down my life, but he knew that it was the only way I could win my bride.*

*The impact of his words hit me: I would allow myself to be killed in her place. I would take the punishment and the blame for my beloved's unfaithfulness, and I would allow my enemies to inflict their evil upon me. To save my beloved from having to endure a torturous death, I agreed to the plan.*

*I know that this will mean something much worse than death by stoning; more than they care about punishing my beloved for her waywardness, the trickster and his cohorts will enjoy watching me die like a hardened criminal. I have gone to the authorities and have offered to take my beloved's place. They have readily agreed.*

## PRACTICAL APPLICATION

Real love is such a wonderful gift of God. He designed love as something we are meant to enjoy. Because He loves you, it is possible for you to be happy and know that there is at least one Somebody who adores you, cares about you, and is your biggest fan.

Love is reassuring and is a source of great comfort. Love can calm the raging storm in your life. Sharing a life together is the greatest experience two people can have. Yet one of the great mysteries of life is why some people make the people who love them pay such a high price to do so.

The sad reality is that there are far too many people who have no idea of what real love is. They spend their entire lives inflicting pain on others. They hurt those around them without feeling any remorse.

Love is not only a characteristic of a person; it is also an emotion—a strong and powerful emotion.

When you feel that emotion for a person, you might begin to develop and display an unconditional commitment to him or her. That's love.

Many people are so selfish, greedy, and wicked that they have no capacity to appreciate the wonderful gift of love. Their concept of love is having a person give them what they want when they want it. This attitude is so strong in today's society that some children are now as crass as street-dwelling adults. There is a prevailing mind-set in people today that makes them feel that they have a right to be catered to.

They are not timid about receiving, but they loathe the very thought of giving back. They will wear out their welcome and think nothing of the consequences. They will take and take and take. When one supply runs out, they will move on to their next victim. Theirs is a profoundly demonic attitude.

This selfish mind-set breeds all kinds of evil behavior. It is not unusual to hear teenagers who have committed gross crimes saying how unmoved they are about what they did. Sexual immorality is accepted as a normal way of living in our society. Virtue, honor, and respect are often considered to be signs of weakness.

Of course, not everyone thinks or acts in this way. The problem is, however, that there are so many people laboring under a selfish, destructive, and wicked mind-set that it is almost certain that a caring person will get involved with an uncaring person. The results are broken hearts and dysfunctional families.

Those who do know what real love is are overwhelmed by feelings of betrayal and disappointment when their love is rejected and abused. When a loving person is abused, the pain he or she feels is severe. The selfish spouse or friend cannot understand that he or she is causing this kind of pain. These two kinds of people have great conflict in their relationships.

When you give your heart to someone, you've given him or her the essence of who you are. You want your feelings to be taken care of and your offering of love to be valued.

When you do know what love is, you not only want to give it away, you also want to receive it, too. You yearn to have someone who feels about you the way you feel about him or her. When you love someone and that person doesn't love you back, your heart aches. You cannot help feeling this way, either.

People who are not involved in a painful love relationship often wonder how unrequited love can hurt so badly. They quickly say that they would react differently in such situations, and they are probably correct in their statements, but they also reveal that they do not love.

It is impossible to really love someone and not be affected by his or her actions. If the person responds positively to you, there is no greater joy. If he or she rejects you, the pain is intense, deep-seated, and long-lasting.

When your love is spurned, you think about the situation all the time. The rejection affects your ability to work, to relate to other people, and to sleep at night. Your mind is racing, trying to discover a solution to your problem. If you find no answers, after a time you may look for drastic measures to resolve the situation.

But true love, though it will feel intense pain when it is rejected, will not always resort to drastic measures. When the true love of God was rejected by humanity, He was patient and merciful, proving His loving-kindness over and over again. Let me explain in more detail.

### The Loving-kindness of Our God

All of us have sinned (Romans 3:23), and our sin has separated us from our Creator. Yet God loved us with such a perfect love that He was willing to bear the punishment of our sin, in the person of His Son, Jesus Christ, in order to restore us to communion with Himself. God's most loving gesture toward us has been the sending of His Son to us. He knew that the only way to win us back to Him would be for Him to die for us, to take our penalty upon Himself.

God's heart is broken again and again because we reject His love and affection. In Matthew 23:37, Christ Himself wept over Jerusalem and lamented that if the Israelites had received Him, He would have given them His all. God wants to give His all to each of His children, including you and me.

Even before the death of Christ on the cross, God made many attempts to draw His people back to Him, though they continually went astray. The story of Hosea typifies the struggle that God has had over the ages with His children. It is similar to the jealous lover's story. God specifically commanded Hosea to marry a harlot as an example to Israel: *"Go, take to yourself a wife of harlotry...for the land commits flagrant harlotry, forsaking the* LORD*"* (Hosea 1:2). Gomer, the harlot who became Hosea's wife, deserted him and sought other lovers. In spite of the depth of her sin, Hosea went and bought back his wife from the auction block, just as the jealous lover had to send his servants to buy back his beloved. (See Hosea 3:1–2.)

# A Man of Sorrows

So many of God's children, like Gomer, continually run after other "lovers," or gods. They stray from Him and pursue worldly things. Nevertheless, the Lord remains faithful and loving. Because of His endless love, He will ultimately save and restore those who stray from Him. *"How can I give you up...? How can I surrender you, O Israel?"* (Hosea 11:8), He asks.

When God sent His Son to die for us, He bridged the gap between Himself and mankind once and for all. But even after we've received Christ as our Savior, we can go astray from Him. God sends His Holy Spirit as a messenger to us, trying to draw us back to Himself.

My dear believer, let me remind you of a few words that the apostle Paul wrote: *"I determined to know nothing among you except Jesus Christ, and Him crucified"* (1 Corinthians 2:2). For years this statement puzzled me, until I discovered the real message of the Gospel. There is nothing more important for us to know than that Jesus died for us.

Theologically speaking, the death of Christ accomplished so much—atonement, redemption, justification, and so on. It makes a fascinating study, to be sure. From purely a perspective of love, however, the death of Jesus proves just how much He cares for us. He was willing to make the supreme sacrifice in order to prove His devotion to us and to save us from eternal separation from God; He was willing to undergo the death penalty and endure God's wrath for our sin. This is the message of Romans 5:8: *"But God commendeth his love toward us, in that, while we were yet sinners, Christ died for us"* (KJV). The word *"commendeth"* is the translation of the Greek word *sunistao* and means "to show, prove, establish, and exhibit." Jesus went to extraordinary measures to get our attention. He didn't talk love; He lived it.

Therefore, in our devotion to Him, we must not concentrate on His temporal gifts alone. Praising Him because He paid the rent, fed us, and clothed us is nice, but the real blessing is that He died so that we could live eternally. *"For the wages of sin is death, but the free gift of God is eternal life in Christ Jesus our Lord"* (Romans 6:23). Bless Him for that today and for the rest of your life!

### A PRAYER

*Dear Lord Jesus, one cannot read the Scriptures, especially Isaiah 53, without stopping to thank You for Your gracious love for us all. I cannot imagine how You must have felt when You died for a people who didn't care about You. I am amazed that You would care enough for me to die for me.*

*Lord, forgive us for being so concerned about the blessings You give us and not about the sacrifice You made for us. Help us to put first things first. Most of all, Lord, may we ever praise You for not giving up on us. In Jesus' name, I pray. Amen.*

*Chapter Eleven*

# *The Mystery Is His Story*

*Chapter Eleven*

# The Mystery Is
# His Story

*Forasmuch then as the children are partakers of flesh
and blood, he also himself likewise took part of the
same; that through death he might destroy him that had
the power of death, that is, the devil; and deliver them
who through fear of death were all their
lifetime subject to bondage.
—Hebrews 2:14–15 KJV*

The detective had listened with great interest to the tragic epic the victim's father
had told. He marveled at the details, but it
hadn't made sense to him when the father read,

from the journal, that his son had decided to take the penalty for his beloved's crime and be put to death. This whole case had been different enough, and now it appeared that it involved an act of incomprehensible sacrifice and unfathomable love. How could this be?

The detective stopped the father in mid-sentence to ask the obvious question: "Why did your son decide to endure another's punishment? There were other women who could have made him happy. And I must admit, sir, that you don't seem too grieved about his passing." The detective was beginning to suspect that maybe the father, for some strange reason, had wanted to get rid of his son.

The father was unmoved and showed no signs of stress.

"Yes, detective, I realize it does seem as though I am too calm under the circumstances. But you must hear me out, and then it will all make sense to you." So the father resumed his son's story.

"After my son wrote in his journal what I just read to you, he didn't have much time left. He went to his bride, so that he could tell her what he planned to do. They did not meet in their gardens the way they once had. Instead, they met in a public place.

"My son's love for his bride was so great. He wanted simply to take her into his arms and forget what was about to happen. But she needed to know that he would do everything he could to win her heart again. As clearly as he could, he explained that he was going to take her place so that she would not have to die. She didn't understand how he could do such a thing, or why.

"He said, 'I will be back for you; wait for me, and we will be reunited. But first I must be delivered into the hands of my enemies.' As he was saying this, several guards grabbed him and snatched him away from his beloved. It was time.

"My son knew that his beloved was a weak person. He said that she was fragile, like a flower that blooms for a short season and then is no more. He was frustrated because she was so unfaithful while he was away preparing for their future. He wanted so much for her and had planned a wonderful life for them both. He had promised to be with her always and to give her things that she'd never had before and could not even imagine having.

"When he first heard about her unfaithfulness, my son was distraught. We talked about what he should do. We agreed that even though he was angry, he should try to get her back.

"He humbled himself and sent his servants to find her and bring her back to her home. For a while it seemed that she would be faithful to my son and would wait for his return, but just about the time we were ready to announce the start of the marriage ceremony, she would run off again.

"He was very patient. He tried everything to convince her that she was better off with him than with the strange man she gave herself to. But the more he tried, the more she seemed determined to resist his efforts.

"Now, I know you police types see so much of the worst of society. To you, leaving her and finding someone else to love seems as if it would have been a reasonable solution to the problem. You only consider the outward appearance of things, and so, in your mind, his bride didn't deserve him and he was too good for her.

"My son, however, is like his father in every respect. In fact, when you see him, you see me. We love unconditionally, and our love never fails. He knew that while his bride seemed unredeemable on the outside, she had a heart that could be touched."

The detective started to speak, but the father stopped him. "I know what you're going to ask, so just keep listening," he said. "You are wondering, if her heart was so able to be touched, why didn't she respond after repeated attempts by my son to win her? That is a good question. You would think that showing her that much kindness would cause her to have a tender spirit toward him.

"Certainly, on more than one occasion, he made it very easy for her to change. He offered to abundantly pardon her and forgive her if she would just change her wicked ways and repent. But for so long she would not take on the responsibility of repenting for her sin.

"Interestingly, repentance is the key to this part of the story. Let me explain. Most people think of repenting as changing your mind. Changing your mind is not enough. The word *repent* means 'to change the manner in which you come to conclusions.'

"For instance, a man who steals something and gets caught will change his mind about stealing, but only because he has to face the consequences of his actions. That's not repentance. The thief merely altered his decision about stealing based upon the consequences. He would steal again as soon as he figured out a way to steal without getting caught. So then, the fact that he changed his mind has no bearing on his future actions. His mind is still made up to be a thief.

"Therefore, repentance is much more than a person's just changing his mind. The key is changing the way he processes information and draws conclusions. Until a person reprograms the way he thinks, he will react in new circumstances in the same way he always has.

"Before I tell you why my son took the penalty upon himself and why I'm not lamenting his departure, let me finish telling you about his bride. After so many cycles of her leaving, his retrieving, their reconciling, and then her leaving again, my son started asking himself some questions.

"First, if she had a heart that could be touched, and if she was not completely beyond the reach of his love, why was she so persistent in running after that strange man—that trickster?

"Second, why did she allow herself to be abused in the manner she did? The man she ran off with was no good and treated her badly. My son, on the other hand, treated her as if she were a queen. There had to be an explanation.

"Sometimes the obvious can be looking right at you, but because you're used to seeing things in a certain way, you miss it. It was obvious that, in some ways, my son's problem was the other man and not the bride. Not only was she refusing to change her ways, but she was also the victim of the trickster's continual harassment. She needed deliverance from both her inclinations to evil and from the power of the trickster.

"The trickster had found a technique that was better than fighting with my son directly. The trickster knew that the best way to torment him was to harass his bride.

"However, harassment alone isn't enough to account for the irrational behavior of the bride. If you look carefully at her lifestyle, you will see that she was acting as an abused person would act.

"On one occasion she told my son, 'I know in my mind that I should be following your directions and enjoying your goodness to me. The problem is that my evil nature is stronger than my mind. I want to do right, and I think about it all the time. However, whenever I try to stay with you, I feel myself being drawn away from you, and before I can catch myself, I am doing the very thing you said not to do.'

"Her weak nature led her to be unfaithful to my son, but the main problem was her fear of death. The trickster saw that he could control her by her fear of death. He told her that if she didn't keep coming to him, he would make sure that she was stoned to death for her adultery. She tried to be brave and stand, but she was weak.

"So then, no matter how many times my son sent servants to get her, she was still in bondage to the other man because of her fear of him. Because she didn't fully accept and receive my son's love, she was unable to make a commitment to him. She needed a true change of heart.

"You can imagine how depressed she must have felt. She started out in life rejected by her own mother and left to die in a pool of her own blood. As she was growing up, she was teased constantly about her appearance. People said she was ugly. Her brothers treated her like an intruder into their family. They told her that she would never amount to anything.

"Then, for one brief moment, somebody showed her kindness. But even that became torment, because the trickster threatened to report her to the authorities immediately if she kept seeing her jealous lover.

"She felt that life, for her, was continuously painful and would come to a painful end. Many times she cried all night long, called herself a wretched woman, and wondered who could deliver her from her fear of death.

"You can understand, then, why she felt helpless and that she was no good. She had no esteem for herself because, in her mind, she had no future. My son could not leave her in this condition. She needed something to live for—hope, and deliverance from her fear of death.

"You know from the journal that my son and I talked about his bride for three hours. He struggled with some of the things I had told him to do, not because he was a disobedient son, but because of the supreme sacrifice it required of him.

"Sometime during that last hour, he became calm and said to me, 'Father, let your will, not mine, be done.' It was at that moment that he became willing to endure the penalty of his bride's adultery. She would not have to be punished, after all.

"My son, the jealous lover, left our meeting with peace in his spirit. As I mentioned earlier, he went right to his bride, to tell her of his plans. While he was explaining things to her, the authorities, who were friends of the trickster, came and took him away. My son surrendered himself into their hands. The trickster and his people made him carry a cross to the place of his death. They inflicted the bruises you saw on his body, the cuts, and all the other signs of abuse.

"After a day of torture, the trickster instructed his people to leave my son to die on the cross. Then the executioners were told to inflict the mortal wound. But by the time they got to my son, he was already dead. He had already surrendered his life for his bride.

"I was there when my son was crucified, but I could not watch. I could not bear to see my son in such a condition. But his bride was watching with fixed attention. She had followed him to see what would happen and to see if he had been telling her the truth about dying in her place. At one point, I looked at her and could see that her eyes were full of tears. The sadness that darkened her face told me that she was recognizing the significance of her lover's death and the wrong that she had done.

"My son was not crazy, nor did he have a death wish. My son loved life; in fact, there was so much life in him that his life brought light to others. My son didn't die for nothing. Instead, he died to prove his love and to free his bride from the trickster's power.

"He had to show his bride that there are some things in life more important than living—and one of those things was giving her deliverance and freedom. Now that he had died for her, he wanted her to know that she didn't have to fear death, the negative comments of people, or the future.

"Most of all, he wanted her to know just how much he loved her. He was not like the other people in her life who had left her and disappointed her. He was so much interested in her that he was willing to die for her.

"My son knew the thoughts that he had for her, thoughts of peace and not evil, thoughts of bringing her into the things that he had planned for her all along. You see, the mystery is his story. When my son died, he forever changed the balance of power in the kingdom. His death destroyed the power of death over his bride. She would not have to die for her sin, because the punishment for the sin had already been administered. Thus, the trickster could no longer threaten her with death. The sting of death was gone, and the grave could no longer claim victory."

The detective shook his head in amazement. He had to tell this story, but would people believe him? There was one final question that needed to be answered.

"I understand how the sting of death is gone, as far as the bride is concerned," said the detective, "but what about your son? You still haven't answered why you are not remorseful about his departure. He definitely sounds like a wonderful person. If I were you, I would be in deep mourning."

The father, with a twinkle in his eye, asked the detective a question: "Detective, how many days have you been investigating this case?"

The detective replied, "Three days."

The father asked him, "Have you heard of the writ of habeas corpus?"

"Of course," the detective replied. "It is one of the most important doctrines of law, order, and justice. The term means 'to have a body.' In our common interpretation, it means that if you do not have a dead body to show, you do not have a case."

There was a faint hint of a smile on the father's face as he instructed the young, dedicated, and patient detective to remove the lid on his son's grave.

Eager to learn more, the detective did as the father instructed. The grave was empty! The detective turned around to question the father about it. But the father was gone.

"This case is continually taking another turn," the detective thought to himself. "I know why the jealous lover died, and I know who was behind his death, but now the body of the jealous lover is missing! Did the authorities move the body? Did someone steal it?" Questions seemed to flood the detective's mind. He walked back to his office, deep in thought, wondering if the case of the jealous lover would ever be completely solved.

## PRACTICAL APPLICATION

The discovery of the details of what Christ did for us all at Calvary is incomparably better than the discovery of electricity or other discoveries that the world honors. Yet, tragically, it is too often overlooked. Earlier I drew you to the statement of

## The Mystery Is His Story

Paul in 1 Corinthians 2:2: *"For I determined to know nothing among you except Jesus Christ, and Him crucified."* It is interesting to me that he didn't say, "Except Jesus Christ the healer and miracle worker." While Jesus was those things and more, Paul focused entirely on the Lord's work at Calvary.

The apostle Paul had a reason for doing so. In a sense, almost everything else that Christ did, in one way or another, could have been done or had been done by someone else in the kingdom. But what He did at Calvary was uniquely His work. He was the only One who could do it and who did do it.

It is always a blessing to review the substitutionary work of Christ on the cross. Upon Him was laid the iniquity of us all, and because of His wounds we were healed (Isaiah 53:5–6). Isaiah 53 is a superlative report of that event on the cross; it gives us a vivid description of Christ's sacrifice for us. Reading it helps us to appreciate the deep love of Christ. Reading the Living Bible's version of this passage is especially helpful. But let's look at Hebrews 12:2 before reading the passage in Isaiah 53.

*Keep your eyes on Jesus, our leader and instructor. He was willing to die a shameful death on the cross because of the joy he knew*

*would be his afterwards; and now he sits in
the place of honor by the throne of God.*
*(Hebrews 12:2 TLB)*

What joy would provoke anyone, even Jesus,
to willingly subject himself to the horrific death of
crucifixion? Isaiah 53 answers this question:

*But it was the Lord's good plan to bruise him
and fill him with grief. However, when his
soul has been made an offering for sin, then
he shall have a multitude of children, many
heirs. He shall live again, and God's pro-
gram shall prosper in his hands. And when
he sees all that is accomplished by the an-
guish of his soul, he shall be satisfied; and
because of what he has experienced, my righteous Servant shall make many to be counted
righteous before God, for he shall bear all
their sins. Therefore, I will give him the honors of one who is mighty and great because he
has poured out his soul unto death. He was
counted as a sinner, and he bore the sins of
many, and he pled with God for sinners.*
*(Isaiah 53:10–12 TLB)*

Obviously, the answer is that the benefits
outweighed the drawbacks. In this passage, we see
that Jesus had a number of positive results of His
suffering, including honor from God the Father

and many heirs—all those who put their trust in Him and become children of God.

My purpose in this book has been to present the gospel message of the Cross from God's point of view. As I said in the Introduction, the mysteries associated with this message lead us to ask questions such as, Why did Christ die? Couldn't He have better served the kingdom alive? What good did His death do? And if His death was required to pay for our redemption, wasn't the price too high?

The Scriptures declare God's sovereignty and tell us that He created all things. Therefore, if God is sovereign and has the power to speak things into existence, why did Christ have to die for us? Couldn't He just have declared us righteous and been done with it?

Our God never operates inefficiently, and He never makes mistakes. Clearly, the fact that He didn't just declare us righteous indicates that He knew it would not have been an effective or even optional way to do things.

Let's explore why that wouldn't have been effective. First, sin is a violation of God's holiness and must be punished. Throughout the Old Testament, a blood sacrifice was always necessary to atone for the sins of mankind. In the New Testament, God did not change His policy. A blood sacrifice was still required to atone for sin, but in Christ, the atonement was made once and for all.

According to Romans 6:23, *"the wages of sin is death"*; we deserved death because of our sin. (See also Romans 5:12.) Yet God loved us enough to send His Son to die in our place, and now *"the free gift of God is eternal life in Christ Jesus our Lord"* (Romans 6:23). Our salvation is through Him.

We could better understand the full measure of Jesus' sacrifice at Calvary if we redefined our concept of salvation. For too many people, *salvation* is a synonym for *rescue*.

True, Jesus did rescue us, but He did much more than just rescue us from punishment for our sins. It is not always necessary to jump in the ocean to rescue someone from drowning. A lifeboat could be sent, or a raft could be thrown to the person. Jesus didn't just rescue us by tossing us a lifeline. Rather, He saved us by becoming what we are—though without sin—so that we can become what He is. He really did jump in the ocean to rescue us from sin! Because of this, *"we do not have a high priest who cannot sympathize with our weaknesses, but One who has been tempted in all things as we are, yet without sin"* (Hebrews 4:15).

The gruesome death of Christ on the cross shows us many things. First, it demonstrates the awesome terror of the Lord and His utter hatred of sin. Romans 8:32 states, *"He...did not spare His own Son."* If He would do this to His own Son because of sin, what will He do to those who refuse to accept His grace?

The death of Christ also displays His supreme love for us, just as the death of the jealous lover displayed his love for his bride. The pain and agony inflicted on Jesus should have been our punishment. But God loved us so much that He allowed His Son to suffer the full brunt of His wrath on our behalf. Moreover, it was God Himself who took our punishment through the person of His Son Jesus Christ. Second Corinthians 5:19 says, *"God was in Christ reconciling the world to Himself."* Likewise, the jealous lover endured the pain of death so that his bride would no longer have to fear it.

In Christ, *"He...who knew no sin* [was made] *to be sin on our behalf, that we might become the righteousness of God in Him"* (verse 21). That's love.

*Chapter Twelve*

# *Hope for the Future*

*Chapter Twelve*

# Hope for the Future

Three days after the death of the jealous lover, the detective had gone to the grave to search for more evidence that would solve his case. There he had encountered the victim's father, who had explained some things, but not everything.

Later that same day, the beloved also went to the grave to mourn the death of her lover. Remembering how she had hurt him by her unfaithfulness, she was distraught at the thought that she would never see him again—would never get a final chance to ask for his forgiveness. When she reached the grave, she discovered that the lid had been lifted, and she saw that the grave was empty! What a frightening moment that was for her. "Oh, what has happened?" she exclaimed. "Where is his body? I must go and find out what has happened! Somebody has to know!"

She ran from the burial site and through the streets, looking for anyone who might know what had become of the jealous lover's body. Some people scoffed in disbelief at her story, but others went to see the empty grave. Everyone in the town knew about the death of the jealous lover, so it was not difficult for the bride to find people who were interested in what might have happened since. Some people began to spread the news, but no one knew what had happened to the body.

Running from place to place, and nearly in a panic, the bride was shocked when she ran right into the jealous lover! Her shock at having run into him turned immediately into rejoicing. "You're alive! Oh, you're alive!" she cried as she ran into his arms.

The jealous lover held her for a long moment. Then he stood back and smiled, taking her hands in his. She saw that he bore the marks of death on his wrists and his feet, but everything else about him was even more beautiful than before. "I have returned, my love," he said, "just as I promised. I have taken your penalty upon myself to prove my love for you. The power of my love for you has brought me back from the dead. Will you marry me?"

She replied, "Oh, yes! I am so sorry for the way I treated you. Because of your great love for me, I want to live with you forever." She was overwhelmed with joy that the jealous lover was alive. "I will go immediately and prepare." At long last, the wedding preparations were begun, and the lovers would soon be joined in perfect unity.

\* \* \*

While the news of the upcoming ceremonies spread through the town, the detective was sitting in his office, still pondering what might have happened to the jealous lover's body. He recalled the empty grave and the sudden disappearance of the jealous lover's father. "Who would have moved the body? Or did someone steal it?" he kept asking himself. "I have to find out what happened, and I'm going to find someone who knows."

Grabbing his coat and setting out to find the jealous lover's father, the detective was rather distracted by his thoughts, but he noticed that the streets were crowded with people who were causing a commotion. "Something must have happened here, and I bet it has something to do with this jealous lover," thought the detective. He approached a small group of people who had gathered.

"What's going on here?" he inquired.

"Haven't you heard, detective? Don't you pay any attention?" The questions came from all sides. "The man who was crucified a few days ago has risen from his grave and is now making wedding plans! We hear it was the power of his love that gave him life again. Can you believe that?"

A smile came across the detective's face, and he said, "Yes, if it involves the jealous lover, I can believe it." Then he thought, "He rose again out of the power of his love. Well, isn't that something? Someday soon, I'm going to have to meet this jealous lover in person." Seeing now why the grave was empty, the detective knew that the case had been solved, and he believed that its ramifications would be felt for years to come.

## PRACTICAL APPLICATION

There is even more to Christ's death than what I have told you so far. His death accomplished more than just our redemption (paying the price to win us) and salvation (rescuing us from the Enemy). His sacrifice also delivered us from the bondage of sin and the fear of death.

## Hope for the Future

Second Timothy 1:10 states that Jesus Christ *"abolished death, and brought life and immortality to light through the gospel."* What does this mean to you and me? In practical terms, it means that Jesus has offered us the gift of eternal life and has destroyed the fear of death. We no longer have to be bound by that fear when we are trusting in God! Let's look at Hebrews 2.

> *Since then the children share in flesh and blood, He Himself likewise also partook of the same, that through death He might render powerless him who had the power of death, that is, the devil; and might deliver those who through fear of death were subject to slavery all their lives.*  (Hebrews 2:14–15)

Through His death, Christ released *"those who through fear of death were subject to slavery all their lives."* Our hope is therefore secure in Him!

Since the fall of man, Satan had made slaves of people through their fear of death. But through His own sacrificial death and glorious resurrection, Jesus conquered death and nullified the power of the Devil over our lives. He took the keys of death, hell, and the grave from the Devil. (See Revelation 1:18.) Now, because of Jesus, believers no longer have to live in fear, and the power of the Devil over them has been cancelled. Because of Christ's life within them, they can now live in the will of God as they never could have done by their own power.

The resurrection of our Lord is the greatest miracle in history. Christ had been brutally beaten and placed on a cross to die like a criminal, but after three days in the tomb, He rose again. He appeared to His disciples and declared that all power in heaven and in earth was in His hands. (See Matthew 28:18.) He appeared to His disciples to prove that He was alive again and to commission them to continue His work in the world. What's more, He has promised to return for His church. (See John 14:2–3.) Like the jealous lover and his bride, we are now preparing for the wedding ceremonies that will take place at the Marriage Supper of the Lamb, when we will be united with Him for eternity. (See Revelation 19:7–9; 21:2, 9–11.) This is what we are eagerly looking forward to! (See 2 Timothy 4:8.)

Jesus is our Champion; He conquered all fear in our lives. If death wasn't enough to stop Jesus or hinder His work or effectiveness, then your problems and cares are not too complicated for Him.

I realized all of this when the Lord saved my life on that cold, winter day at Lake Tawakani. He took away my fear of death and set me free from the bondage that the Devil had had me in for so long. I saw that all of my problems, hurts, and disappointments are manageable by the Lord. The same applies to you. If death couldn't stop Jesus, then your wayward son or daughter, your spouse's drug abuse problem, your unemployment, or your medical condition cannot stop Him from causing *"all things to work together for good"* (Romans 8:28).

Above all, as I wrote earlier, we need to love Jesus not only for what He does for us, but also for who He is. Jesus is more than a problem solver, automobile repairman, or rent subsidizer. He's more than a matchmaker, grant approver, or travel agent who books trips to heaven. He's more than a debt liquidation specialist, grief manager, or food pantry operator.

Jesus is the Lover of your soul and has deep passion and zeal for what belongs to Him. He will do anything for you and asks for so little in return. What He does ask for is your total commitment to Him. He wants to meet you in the cool of the evening just to hear the sound of your voice. He wants to take care of every aspect of your needs. He wants to take you to a higher level in Him. He wants to show you His glory and to glorify you. Let Him!

Most of all, He wants you to love Him more than anything else, for His name is Jealous (Exodus 34:14). Trust Him at all costs, and wait for

Him. For *"He who began a good work in you will perfect it until the day of Christ Jesus"* (Philippians 1:6).

## A PRAYER

*Dear Father, we are humbled by the magnitude of Your concern and love for us. Help us to lift You up in our hearts and seat You on the throne of our souls. Help us to love You in every situation.*

*Keep us in the center of Your will, and teach us Your ways. Guide us with Your eye. Help us, Lord, to learn how to love You more. Let us rest in Your care.*

*Most of all, thank You, Lord, for setting us free from slavery to sin, fear, and the Enemy, and for uniting us to You as our Bridegroom, the Lover of our souls. Come quickly, Lord; we're waiting for You. In Jesus' name, we pray. Amen.*